Beginning PBR Texturing

Learn Physically Based Rendering with Allegorithmic's Substance Painter

Abhishek Kumar

Apress®

Beginning PBR Texturing

Abhishek Kumar
Varanasi, Uttar Pradesh, India

ISBN-13 (pbk): 978-1-4842-5898-9   ISBN-13 (electronic): 978-1-4842-5899-6
https://doi.org/10.1007/978-1-4842-5899-6

Managing Director, Apress Media LLC: Welmoed Spahr
Acquisitions Editor: Spandana Chatterjee
Development Editor: Laura Berendson
Coordinating Editor: Divya Modi

Cover designed by eStudioCalamar

Cover image designed by Pixabay

Distributed to the book trade worldwide by Springer Science+Business Media New York, 233 Spring Street, 6th Floor, New York, NY 10013. Phone 1-800-SPRINGER, fax (201) 348-4505, e-mail orders-ny@springer-sbm.com, or visit www.springeronline.com. Apress Media, LLC is a California LLC and the sole member (owner) is Springer Science + Business Media Finance Inc (SSBM Finance Inc). SSBM Finance Inc is a **Delaware** corporation.

For information on translations, please e-mail rights@apress.com, or visit www.apress.com/rights-permissions.

Apress titles may be purchased in bulk for academic, corporate, or promotional use. eBook versions and licenses are also available for most titles. For more information, reference our Print and eBook Bulk Sales web page at www.apress.com/bulk-sales.

Any source code or other supplementary material referenced by the author in this book is available to readers on GitHub via the book's product page, located at www.apress.com/978-1-4842-5898-9. For more detailed information, please visit www.apress.com/source-code.

Printed on acid-free paper

*To Mom; Dad; Prof. B K Prasad; Usha Sinha;
and my beloved wife, Alka, for 11 fantastic years of
marriage and many more to come. To my daughter,
Rishika Ryan, and my son, Shivaay Singh Ryan,
who were both in a hurry to enter the world.
I love you all.*

Table of Contents

About the Author xi

About the Technical Reviewer xiii

Acknowledgments xv

Introduction xvii

Chapter 1: What Is Our Goal in This Book? 1

Want a Career as a Game Developer? 2

    Game Studios 2

    Tools 4

What's in This Book? 5

    Chapter 1: What Is Our Goal in This Book? 5

    Chapter 2: Graphics in the Game Industry 5

    Chapter 3: Texturing Workflow 5

    Chapter 4: Texturing Games vs. Texturing Movies 6

    Chapter 5: PBR Texturing vs. Traditional Texturing 6

    Chapter 6: Substance Suite and Substance Painter 7

    Chapter 7: Hardware Specifications for Your Computer 7

    Chapter 8: Painters' Graphical User Interface 7

    Chapter 9: Viewport Navigation in Painter 8

    Chapter 10: Setting Up a Project 8

    Chapter 11: Baking and the Importance of Mesh Maps 8

    Chapter 12: Working with Materials, Layers, and Masks 9

Chapter 13: Working with Procedural Maps 9

Chapter 14: Substance Anchors 10

Chapter 15: Rendering with Iray 10

Chapter 16: Integrating with Blender, Maya and Marmoset 10

Chapter 17: Rendering a Portfolio 11

Chapter 18: Integration with Unreal Engine 4...11

Chapter 19: Tips and Tricks of Substance Painter 11

How to Best Use This Book 12

Chapter 2: Graphics in the Game Industry...13

Concept of Computer Graphics 13

Uses of Computer Graphics 16

Substance Suite in the Industry...21

Visualization Basics 22

What Is PBR?...27

Game Engines 28

Chapter 3: Texturing Workflow 31

Game Texturing Pipeline 32

Useful Tips for Texture Artists 34

What Is UV Mapping?...35

Types of Textures 35

Chapter 4: Texturing Games vs. Texturing Movies............................39

Texture Pipeline for Movies..40

Texture Pipeline for Games 40

Common Pipelines and Similarities for Games and Films 41

Chapter 5: PBR Texturing vs. Traditional Texturing 43

Texturing Using 3D Painting Applications 44

Texturing Using 2D Painting Applications 45

PBR Textures in the Gaming Industry...45

Chapter 6: Substance Suite and Substance Painter 47

Why Substance? 47

Uses of Other Substance Suite Applications 49

    Substance Source 49

    Substance Alchemist..50

    Substance Designer 52

Chapter 7: Hardware Specifications for Your Computer 55

GPU vs. CPU 55

Recommended Hardware 57

Chapter 8: Painters' Graphical User Interface 59

The UI and Tools..59

Guide to the Shelf 66

Chapter 9: Viewport Navigation in Painter 71

Keyboard Shortcuts...71

Guide to Commonly Used Tools..74

Chapter 10: Setting Up a Project 77

Getting Started with Substance Painter..77

Project Configuration in Detail 79

Chapter 11: Baking and the Importance of Mesh Maps 81

Introduction to the Baker 82

Uses of Mesh Maps...85

Chapter 12: Working with Materials, Layers, and Masks 89

Materials and Smart Materials...89

Layers and Masks 90

Layer Operations 91

Masks...94

Smart Masks 97

Mask Operations 98

Chapter 13: Working with Procedural Maps...........................105

Filters..105

Applying a Filter..105

Commonly Used Filters..108

Generators 117

Dirt Generator 119

Metal Edge Wear Generator..122

Dripping Rust Generator 124

Auto Stitcher...124

Mask Builder – Legacy and Mask Editor 125

Uses of Grunges and Other Procedural Maps 127

Using Patterns as Height 129

Patterns as Masks...133

Procedural Images as Maps 137

Chapter 14: Substance Anchors 143

What Is an Anchor? 143

Using Anchor Points in a Practical Way..144

Chapter 15: Rendering with Iray 157

Launching the Renderer...158

Renderer Settings 158

Chapter 16: Integrating with Blender, Maya and Marmoset.............165

Low Poly and High Poly Workflow 166

Blender to Substance Workflow..169

Maya to Substance Painter Workflow 174

Importing into Blender, Maya, and Marmoset 176

Exporting from Substance for Use in Blender 176

Exporting from Substance for Use in Maya 181

Exporting from Substance for Use in Marmoset Toolbag 184

Chapter 17: Rendering a Portfolio 187

Integration with Blender 187

Integration with Maya 203

Integration with Marmoset Toolbag 215

Chapter 18: Integration with Unreal Engine 4 221

Exporting to Unreal Engine 4..222

Importing into Unreal Engine 4 225

Chapter 19: Tips and Tricks of Substance Painter 243

Using Brushes and Alphas 243

Creating Stitches..250

Creating Damage Using the Height Channel 251

Index..257

About the Author

 **Dr. Abhishek Kumar** is an assistant professor in the Department of Computer Science at the Institute of Science at Banaras Hindu University. He is an Apple Certified Associate, an Adobe Education Trainer, and Autodesk certified. He is actively involved in the development of animation and design engineering courses for various institutions and universities.

Dr. Kumar has published a number of research papers, covering a wide range of topics in various digital scientific areas (image analysis, visual identity, graphics, digital photography, motion graphics, 3D animation, visual effects, editing, and composition). He holds two patents in the field of design and IoT and has created two inventions related to a pipeline inspection robot to help visually impaired people.

Dr. Kumar has completed professional studies related to animation, computer graphics, virtual reality, stereoscopy, filmmaking, visual effects, and photography from Norwich University of Arts, University of Edinburg, and Wizcraft MIME and FXPHD in Australia. He is passionate about the media and entertainment industry and has directed two animation short films.

Dr. Kumar has trained more than 50,000 students across the globe from 153 countries (top five: India, Germany, United States, Spain, Australia). His alumni have worked on national and international movies such as *Ra-One, Krissh, Dhoom, Life of Pi*, the *Avengers* series, the *Iron Man* series, *GI Joe 3D, 300, Alvin and the Chipmunks, Prince of Persia, Titanic 3D*, the *Transformers* series, *Bahubali* 1 and 2, *London Has Fallen, Warcraft, Aquaman 3D, Alita*, and more.

About the Technical Reviewer

Bhuvnesh Kumar Varshney works as a 3D and visual effects developer with 13+ years of experience in production and product development. His main interests are in character, creature, and facial animation. He has worked at various companies as a team lead and senior artist with the world's leading animation and visual effects studios, including Technicolor, DQ Entertainment, and Anibrain. Currently he works at Yash Raj Films as a senior creature animator.

His notable work on movies, TV series, and commercials include *Wallykazam, Sava, 99 Super Hero, How to Train Your Dragon, Barbie, Penguins of Madagascar, Robot and Monster, Freez, Back at the Barnyard, Mickey & the Roadster Racers, Sheriff Callie's Wild West, Super 4, Tell It to the Bees, Show Dog, Budweiser, Skoda, Norm of the North,* and *Rump and Azwan.* He is currently working on Bollywood movies such as *War, Mardani 2,* and the upcoming movies *Prithviraj* and *Shamshera* from Yash Raj Films.

Email: bhuvnesh3danimator@gmail.com, bhuvnesh@yrfstudios.com

Acknowledgments

It gives me immense pleasure to express my deep sense of gratitude to my mentor Prof. Saket Kushwaha and my PhD supervisor, Dr. Achintya Singhal, associate professor at Banaras Hindu University and my Mentor Prof. Alok Kumar Rai, Professor at Banaras Hindu University who have been the inspiration for this endeavor. Without their encouragement, support, and guidance, this accomplishment would not have been possible.

I would also like to thank Bhuvnesh Varshney, Spandana Chatterjee, Divya Modi, and Laura Berendson for their contributions to publishing this book. Their helpful comments and suggestions resulted in numerous refinements and corrections that improved the quality of this book.

A special thanks to Prof. Ramadevi Nimmanapalli and Bhaskar Bhattacharya for providing unconditional support.

Introduction

This book delves deep into the concepts of physically based rendering (PBR) using Substance Painter. It also covers the integration of PBR textures with various 3D modeling and rendering packages as well as a game engine, in this case, Unreal Engine 4.

PBR-based texturing is in high demand in the video game industry with games becoming more and more graphically realistic. Traditional texturing workflows are rapidly being replaced with fast, procedural texturing suites such as the Substance suite, Quixel DDO Painter, and Mari. Allegorithmic's Substance Painter is an extremely powerful texturing tool that is used by studios worldwide for texturing game assets, environments, and characters. This book covers all the necessary aspects of the software and its general concepts that will help you understand the software better and also guide you through implementing some incredible possibilities. Starting with the theory of physically based rendering, the book moves into the specifics of the Substance applications. Next, it covers baking, material and masks, and procedural texturing. This is followed by instructions for how to integrate with rendering engines, both internal as well as popular external ones. The final chapters reinforce the concepts through practical implementations.

After going through this book, the reader will have complete knowledge of texturing workflows as well as a pipeline for implementing generated textures into the 3D renderer and game engine's real-time renderer.

This book is suitable for beginners to intermediate users in the fields of 3D animation, computer graphics, and game technology. This book is primarily for the students looking for a career in the 3D animation, games, and visual effects industries and those who want to learn to effectively use all the latest industry-standard tools and techniques. This book wraps up by explaining how to create show reel–ready assets using Iray and how to integrate with game, animation, and visual effect industry-standard applications like Blender and Autodesk Maya.

Specifically, in this book you will do the following:

- Learn what's needed to get into game design as a career

- Learn the fundamentals of PBR-based texturing from the ground up

- Learn to integrate PBR textures with game engines

- Learn to integrate with standard 3D modeling and rendering applications such as Maya and Blender

- Learn tips and tricks that will improve your workflow and help you create a production-ready textured model from scratch

CHAPTER 1

What Is Our Goal in This Book?

This book delves deep into the concepts of physically based rendering (PBR) using Substance Painter. It also covers how to integrate PBR textures with various 3D modeling and rendering packages as well as with a game engine, in this case, Unreal Engine 4.

PBR-based texturing is in high demand in the video game industry, with games becoming more and more graphically realistic. Traditional texturing workflows are rapidly being replaced by the fast, procedural texturing suites such as the Substance suite, Quixel DDO Painter, and Mari. Allegorithmic's Substance Painter is an extremely powerful texturing tool that is used by studios worldwide for texturing game assets, environments, and characters. This book covers all the necessary aspects of the software; I'll cover some concepts that will help you understand the software better and also guide you on how to create PBR textures using Substance Painter. Starting with the theory of physically based rendering, the book moves to the specifics of Substance Painter. Next, it covers baking, material and masks, and procedural texturing within Substance Painter. This is followed by how to integrate with rendering engines, both real-time and popular offline ones. The final chapters reinforce the concepts through practical implementations.

After reading this book, you will have complete knowledge of texturing workflows as well as a pipeline for implementing generated textures into a 3D renderer engine and or game engine application's real-time renderer.

© Abhishek Kumar 2020
A. Kumar, *Beginning PBR Texturing*, https://doi.org/10.1007/978-1-4842-5899-6_1

Want a Career as a Game Developer?

The gaming industry is the largest segment within the media and entertainment industry. Currently, the game industry is estimated to be worth $100 billion globally with more than 2.5+ billion gamers across the world; this exceeds the revenue from the film and music segments. In addition, the revenue is expected to grow annually by 2.2 percent, reaching a market volume of $95,388 million by the end of 2024.

For gamers, working in the gaming industry is likely to be their dream job. But it can be difficult for someone who is passionate about gaming to choose the right career path in the game industry. First, you need to find out where you fit in, be it a concept designer, game designer, developer, gameplay tester, level designer, sound engineer, or producer. If you have the right skills and a commitment to the world of video games, the possibilities are endless.

One of the biggest challenges in the game industry is that the technologies and tools rapidly change. Currently, virtual reality and augmented reality games are more popular. Therefore, I recommend you never stop learning about and keeping up-to-date with new technology.

Game Studios

Figure 1-1 and Table 1-1 highlight some of the notable game companies that have been consistently voted to be the best in the world.

Figure 1-1. *Game studios*

Table 1-1. *Notable Game Companies*

Company Name	Location	Notable Games/Platforms
Nintendo	Kyoto (Japan)	*Mario*, *Pokémon*, *The Legend of Zelda*
Valve Corporation	Bellevue, Washington (USA)	*Counter-Strike* series, *Dota 2*, *Day of Defeat* series, *Half-Life* series
Rockstar Games	New York City, New York (USA)	*Grand Theft Auto*, *Red Dead*, *Midnight club*, *Bully*, *Max Payne*
Electronic Arts	Redwood City, California (USA)	*Army of Two* series, *Battlefield* series, *FIFA* series, *The Simpsons* series, *Star Wars* series
Activision Blizzard	Santa Monica, California (USA)	*Call of Duty* series, *Crash Bandicoot* series, *Spyro the Dragon* series, *Tony Hawk* series
Sony Computer Entertainment	Minato, Tokyo (Japan)	PlayStation, PlayStation 2, PlayStation 3, PlayStation 4, PlayStation Vita
Ubisoft	Montreuil (France)	*Assassin's Creed* series, *Far Cry* series, *Just Dance* series, *Tom Clancy* series
Sega Games Co. Ltd	Tokyo (Japan)	*Sonic the Hedgehog*, *Virtua Fighter*, *Phantasy Star*, *Yakuza*, *Total War*
BioWare	Edmonton, Alberta (Canada)	*Mass Effect* series, *Dragon Age* series, *Star Wars: Knights of the Olds*, *Baldur's Gate* series, *Republic* series
Naughty Dog Inc.	Santa Monica, California (USA)	*Crash Bandicoot*, *Jak and Daxter*, *The Last of Us*, *Unchartered*

(*continued*)

Table 1-1. (*continued*)

Company Name	Location	Notable Games/Platforms
Capcom Company	Chuo-Ku, Osaka (Japan)	*Monster Hunter, Resident Evil, Street Fighter*
Microsoft Corporation	Redmond, Washington (USA)	Xbox 360, Xbox One
Bungie Inc.	Bellevue, Washington (USA)	*Pathways into Darkness, Marathon, Halo: Combat Evolved*

Tools

To have a career in the game industry, a key prerequisite is artistic ability. In addition, you probably need to be technically skilled in the use of digital software such as Adobe Photoshop, Autodesk Max, Maya, Z-Brush, Mudbox, and the Substance suite. It also helps to know how to work with game engines such as Cryengine, Corona, GameMaker, Unreal, or Unity (see Figure 1-2).

Figure 1-2. *Tools for game design and development*

What's in This Book?

This book contains 19 chapters covering the following topics.

Chapter 1: What Is Our Goal in This Book?

Chapter Goal: In the chapter you're reading now, you'll learn what each chapter covers and how to best use the book in a practical way to develop your skills.

Specifically, this chapter covers the following:

- Our goal

- Popular game companies

- How to best use this book

Chapter 2: Graphics in the Game Industry

Chapter Goal: In this chapter, you will take a peek at the video game industry. Also, I'll discuss the software used in a production pipeline.

Specifically, this chapter covers the following:

- The concept of computer graphics

- Visualization basics

- What PBR is

- Game render engines/game engines

Chapter 3: Texturing Workflow

Chapter Goal: This chapter discusses the general workflows for preparing a model for texturing. It also covers the importance of UV unwrapping as well as the common problems that can arise while texturing and how to handle them.

Specifically, this chapter covers the following:

- Game texturing pipeline

- What UV mapping is

- The different types of texture maps

Chapter 4: Texturing Games vs. Texturing Movies

Chapter Goal: Here you will learn more about the major differences as well as the similarities between texturing assets for movies and texturing assets for games.

Specifically, this chapter covers the following:

- Texture map fundamentals

- The major differences

- Common pipelines and similarities

Chapter 5: PBR Texturing vs. Traditional Texturing

Chapter Goal: In this chapter, I will discuss the various traditional and modern texturing methods and their pros and cons. This will help you decide which method is best suited for you.

Specifically, this chapter covers the following:

- Texturing using 2D painting applications

- Texturing using 3D texture painting applications

- PBR texturing examples

- PBR versus traditional texturing

Chapter 6: Substance Suite and Substance Painter

Chapter Goal: I'll introduce the four software applications that come with the Substance suite and the different functions of each and where they are used in the industry.

Specifically, this chapter covers the following:

- What Substance Painter is

- Why you should use substances?

- The uses of other Substance suite applications

Chapter 7: Hardware Specifications for Your Computer

Chapter Goal: This chapter discusses the recommended hardware configurations required to run Substance Painter properly.

Specifically, this chapter covers the following:

- GPUs versus CPUs

- Recommended hardware

Chapter 8: Painters' Graphical User Interface

Chapter Goal: All the essential shortcuts and the GUI for Substance Painter are covered in this chapter.

Specifically, this chapter covers the following:

- Main menu

- Sliders

- Toolbars

- Properties

- Texture Set

- Layer Stack

- History

- Shelf

- Display Settings

Chapter 9: Viewport Navigation in Painter

Chapter Goal: In this chapter, you will be introduced to the viewport and all the tools and shelves of Substance Painter.

Specifically, this chapter covers the following:

- Common shortcuts

- A detailed guide to commonly used tools

Chapter 10: Setting Up a Project

Chapter Goal: This chapter covers how to set up a project in Substance Painter and what the correct settings are for doing this.

Specifically, this chapter covers the following:

- Choosing a substance workflow

- Importing a project into Substance Painter

- Configuring projects in detail

Chapter 11: Baking and the Importance of Mesh Maps

Chapter Goal: In this chapter, you will learn about the importance of baking maps and their uses.

Specifically, this chapter covers the following:

- Introduction to the baker

- Baking parameters in Substance Painter

- Uses of different maps created by the baker

Chapter 12: Working with Materials, Layers, and Masks

Chapter Goal: This chapter introduces you to the materials and the robust layer-based workflow that allows the creation of complex materials using masks.

Specifically, this chapter covers the following:

- Introduction to materials and smart materials

- How to build up your material

- Layers and masks

Chapter 13: Working with Procedural Maps

Chapter Goal: In this chapter, I will discuss how to texture procedurally using various maps and filters, and I will discuss more advanced uses of masks.

Specifically, this chapter covers the following:

- Detailed introduction of filters

- Comprehensive introduction of generators

- Uses of grunge and other procedural textures

Chapter 14: Substance Anchors

Chapter Goal: In this chapter, you will now learn about the anchor system of Substance Painter and how powerful it is.

Specifically, this chapter covers the following:

- What an anchor is

- Using an anchor point as a reference

- How to effectively use an anchor

Chapter 15: Rendering with Iray

Chapter Goal: This chapter discusses the internal rendering engine of Substance Painter, Nvidia Iray, and how to render an asset using it.

Specifically, this chapter covers the following:

- What Iray is

- Iray's render settings

- How to export Painter files

Chapter 16: Integrating with Blender, Maya and Marmoset

Chapter Goal: In this chapter, I will discuss the procedure for exporting the created material from Substance Painter to other popular render engines.

Specifically, this chapter covers the following:

- Exporting from Marmoset, Maya, and Blender

- Importing into Marmoset, Maya, and Blender

- Setting up materials in Marmoset, Maya, and Blender

Chapter 17: Rendering a Portfolio

Chapter Goal: In this chapter, I will discuss the process of importing maps in the render engine of your choice and rendering a portfolio-ready image. In our case, we will use the Blender and Marmoset tools.

Specifically, this chapter covers the following:

- Setting up materials in Blender

- Rendering with Blender

- Rendering with the Marmoset tools

Chapter 18: Integration with Unreal Engine 4

Chapter Goal: In this chapter, you will learn about the process of exporting materials for a game engine (Unreal Engine 4, in our case) as well as setting up the material inside the game engine for use.

Specifically, this chapter covers the following:

- Exporting from Unreal Engine 4

- Importing into Unreal Engine 4

- Setting up materials

Chapter 19: Tips and Tricks of Substance Painter

Chapter Goal: In this final chapter, I will discuss some tips and tricks that will help speed up your workflow and help you even further to create something interesting.

Specifically, this chapter covers the following:

- Some general tips

- Integration of Substance Painter with Designer

- Some tricks to use with certain tools

- Substance Painter use in the media and entertainment industry

How to Best Use This Book

As we all know, game development is a mixture of mathematics, computer science, and creative arts, so when you want to learn any tool for game development, practical experience is mandatory.

- Go through each chapter carefully.

- Don't skip any chapters.

- Work through the steps in Substance Painter for the best results.

- Use the resource files provided with the book.

I hope that after reading this you are excited to start your journey into the game industry. In the next chapter, you'll explore how graphics in the video game industry work.

CHAPTER 2

Graphics in the Game Industry

Video game graphics have come a long way since their inception.
The first game ever created was the extremely simple *Pong* tennis game that
was played using primitive graphics consisting of glowing dots and lines
on a cathode ray oscilloscope and two aluminum controllers. Its creator,
American physicist William Higginbotham, did not think it was much at
the time and thought it was just a temporary fad. But what he did not know
was that one day this technology would revolutionize the entertainment
industry. Since then, graphics have gone through a long evolution process
to where they currently are today. Let's explore all the details in this chapter.

Concept of Computer Graphics

Computer graphics (CG) have grown to include the creation, storage, and
manipulation of models and the creation of objects. It is the most effective
way to improve your presentation and communication skills in the form
of graphics objects such as charts, pictures, visualization, and diagrams
instead of traditional text.

In computer graphics, objects are presented as a collection of distinct
picture elements (picture element = *pixel* = pel). Computer graphics
are generated by controlling a pixel (an addressable image element in a
screen), and the control is achieved by setting the intensity and color of

© Abhishek Kumar 2020
A. Kumar, *Beginning PBR Texturing*, https://doi.org/10.1007/978-1-4842-5899-6_2

the pixel, which composes the screen image. *Rasterization* is the process of determining the appropriate pixels to represent graphics or continuous pictures or graphics objects (Figure 2-1).

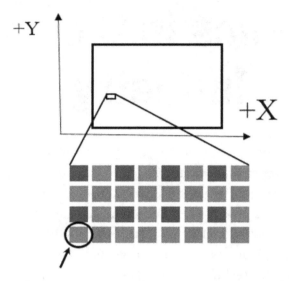

Figure 2-1. *Pixel representation*

Until the early 1980s, computer graphics were costly due to the price of the hardware. When the home PC was introduced, the scenario changed completely. Even small industries could think about producing broadcast-quality output (Figure 2-2).

Because of the growth in three-dimensional (3D) computer graphics, now we have affordable 3D graphics. We can easily create camera-based modeling, build autonomous characters, and generate hyper-realistic environments.

Nowadays several application programs are available to produce computer graphics imagery, either as 2D images, as 3D models, or as animated sequences.

Popular software for the creation of graphics include Corel Draw, Photoshop, AutoCAD, Maya, Max, Cinema4d, Houdini, etc., GKS, DirectX, PostScript, and OpenGL. These are common graphics languages, libraries, and application programming interfaces (APIs). Basically, computer graphics = mathematics + computer science + design.

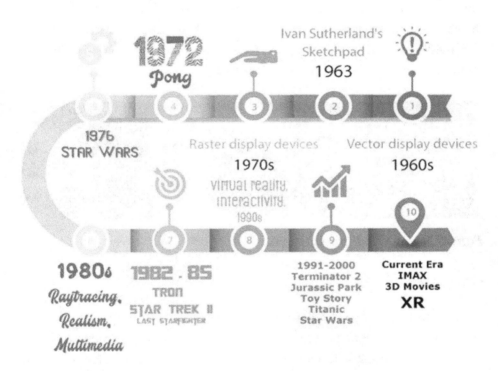

Figure 2-2. *History of computer graphics*

Uses of Computer Graphics

Obvious uses of computer graphics are in art, CGI films, architectural drawings, and graphic designs. In addition, they have made a huge contribution to films, games, and scientist visualization.

Film

Computer graphics are commonly used to make motion pictures, videos, and television shows. Film and video are the two most exciting and fastest-growing areas in the 3D graphics world. 3D graphics are also used to provide many different types of effects, from virtual fire to virtual 3D characters to virtual backgrounds (Figure 2-3).

Figure 2-3. *CGI in films*

Gaming

In the gaming industry, CGI applications are being used for low polygon character modeling or the creation of terrains and architectural backdrops, as shown in Figure 2-4. In fact, Autodesk Max and Maya are used in almost 50 percent of the games that are created today due to the flexibility of the Autodesk programming interface and its powerful modeling and texturing tools. In addition, the new generation of 3D software is able to produce interactive graphics, with approachable extensibility.

Figure 2-4. *Interactive 3D games*

The Autodesk tools Max and Maya are truly open architecture to create premiere 3D content creation tools for next-generation game development such as Microsoft's Xbox and Sony's PlayStation 2. There are several options are available in Autodesk Max; have special hooks specifically for game developers. This makes it easy for game developers to work with vertex colors, export animation data to their game engines, or create low polygon models for use in games.

Visualization

With computer graphics software like Autodesk Maya, Max, and Blender, architects, engineers, and filmmakers can now show their clients exactly how their project will look as an architectural walk-through long before it has ever been built, as shown in Figure 2-5. This saves not only time and money but makes the clients happier as design flaws are much more easily prevented this way.

17

Figure 2-5. *Architectural visualization created in 3D application*

Technical Animation

Technical animation is a field that is similar to visualization. In many instances, this involves the use of hard surface modeling and photorealistic rendering that produce clean, crisp renders of technical and scientific simulations. In general, these renderings and animations are highly accurate and realistic, as shown in Figure 2-6. All 3D applications such as Maya, Max, and Blender have the tools necessary to address this field of work directly out of the box.

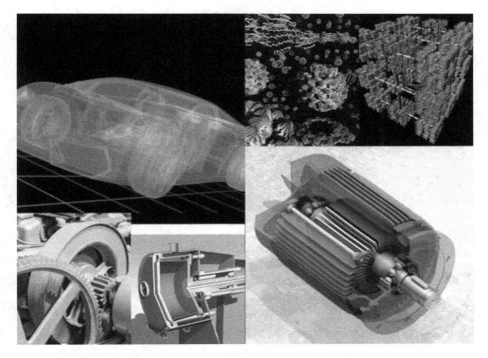

Figure 2-6. *Technical and scientific animation*

Forensic and Medical Animation

Forensic and medical animation was one of the first industries to make use of 3D graphics. In this industry, 3D graphics are used to re-create forensic and medical simulations, as shown in Figure 2-7. In general, these types of animations are low-detail but highly accurate in the timing of the animation. Detail is kept out of the renderings to make them clearer to prospective jurors and expert witnesses.

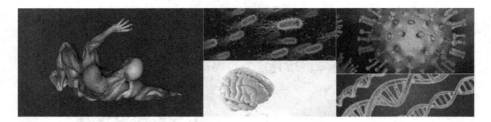

Figure 2-7. *Forensic and medical animation*

Numerous key feature additions and medical animation enhancements complement these major initiatives. A highly tuned animation system allows artists to bring their ideas to life with the most advanced tools for modeling and animating the objects.

Web and Interactive Graphics

Along with specific applications, web element design covers a large part of computer graphics. Graphics are used for interactive web site creations such as realistic shopping malls where you can walk through a store, pick up items, look at them, and eventually purchase them. Nowadays many web sites offer augmented reality (AR), virtual reality (VR), mixed reality (MR), or cross-reality (XR) so buyers can judge the product interactively before deciding whether to purchase it (Figure 2-8).

Figure 2-8. *Graphics layout for web sites (source: lenskart.com, xr.plus, eyerim.com)*

Substance Suite in the Industry

The Substance suite offers an extremely powerful set of texturing tools.
It combines all the necessary tools as a Substance bundle, as shown in
Figure 2-9.

Figure 2-9. *Substance suite*

- Substance Designer (material creation with absolute
  control)

- Substance Painter (painting in 3D in real time)

- Substance Alchemist (the material enthusiast's
  toolbox)

Nowadays the Substance suite is widely used in every industry where
you might find 3D graphics. The applications of Substance are film, design,
gaming, architecture visualization, and transportation (see Figure 2-10).

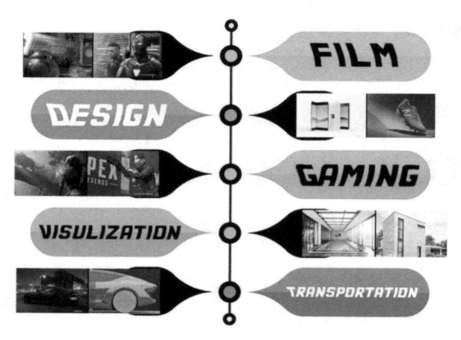

Figure 2-10. *Substance use in different sectors*

Visualization Basics

There are several other distinct processes required to produce 3D computer graphics. Often these must be accomplished in a specific order. This is called a *pipeline*, or sometimes a *production pipeline*. This pipeline is typically divided into three stages, as shown in Figure 2-11.

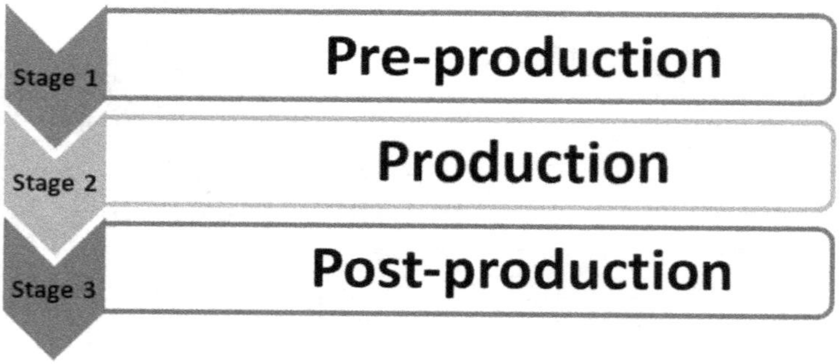

Stage 1 | **Pre-production**

Stage 2 | **Production**

Stage 3 | **Post-production**

Figure 2-11. *Production pipeline*

The process of creating 3D computer graphics is much more complex than what common people think. The framework to produce a 3D CGI can vary depending on the production house pipeline involved and the size and budget of the project. To produce a 3D movie, for example, a large group of technical artists with different skillsets are required. To execute such a complicated process efficiently and affordably, a well-planned and detailed framework is required that will lead to a 3D movie or asset as the final production output.

The pre-production stage is where all the concept designs are completed and transformed into action for the next stage. In the production stage, the concept sketches are converted into 3D design. For the best outcome of this stage, you will do the following tasks:

- Poly engineering/modeling

- Texture mapping

- Lighting

- Rigging/character setup

- Animation

- Dynamics and simulation

- Rendering

- Match-moving

- Compositing

Here are the tasks in more detail:

Modeling: The process of sculpting the geometry in 3D is usually called *modeling*. Modeling requires the ability to study the shape and form of an object to find the most appropriate way to turn it into a model within the computer.

Modeling is generally divided into two categories.

- **Inorganic modeling, also called object modeling**: This includes geometric shapes such as cars, buildings, machines, etc.

- **Organic modeling**: This includes faces, muscles, and skin. By default, the computer model is displayed with a diffuse grayscale appearance.

Texture mapping: To change the outward appearance of a piece of geometry, you need to create good shaders and assign them to pieces of geometry. Shaders are materials with different attributes that control how an object reacts to light and also its environment.

These attributes might include things such as color and surface detail. When you use textures or 2D images to control these attributes to create a texture map for the 3D surface of the model, there is a need to unwrap the model.

Unwrapping is a method to generate a UV map or create a 2D or flat representation of the surface of a 3D model that is used to easily wrap the textures or images. As you can see in Figure 2-12, in the center is the unwrapped UV map of car. This UV map is used as a guide in order to paint the texture. Creating textures to be used in texture mapping is an art form in itself. 2D image manipulation software and real-time 3D texture painting software such as Substance Painter and Mari are now being used in certain industries. These applications allow painting on 3D geometry.

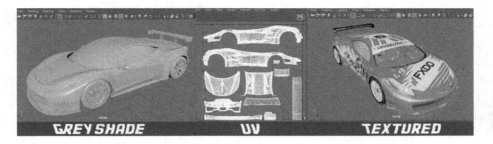

Figure 2-12. *Car texturing*

Lighting: Just like filming anything in real life, scenes must be direct with combinations of lights and lighting techniques. Lighting involves understanding the technicalities of digital lights but also the subjective awareness of how to use lights to set a mood for the storytelling process.

Rigging: Closely associated with animation, rigging takes the bone setup of the geometry and makes it suitable for animation. This can range from simple constraints to a full-character muscle system.

Animation: Animation is the process that brings 3D geometry to life or simple word, Animation is the illusion of motion. 3D animation involves manipulating the physical position of an object over time. In any 3D Animation application time is displayed by a timeline in which each second is divided into frames. Generally in industry, we consider every 24 frames equals to one second.

Dynamics: More specialist parts of the 3D process often appear in the production pipeline. These might include dynamics; physical simulation, such as hair, fur, and cloth; and particles simulation.

Rendering: In the pipeline, rendering is the last process. Rendering is a series of complex calculations converting the digital scene from a camera into a high-quality image or, in the case of animations and an image for every frame, resulting in an image sequence that can be played back as a moving image.

Match-moving: In match-moving, the virtual camera copies the movements of the real world. As you can see in Figure 2-13, It is the perfect match of computer graphics to live-action film.

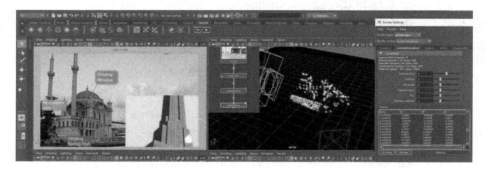

Figure 2-13. *CG live integration*

Compositing: This is the process where renders and live-action can be combined and also augmented into an 2D image.

Computer graphics are used in many different industries, and therefore there are many different flavors of computer graphics. They include commercials, TV shows, games, architectural visualization, product design, and blockbuster movies.

What Is PBR?

A physically based rendering (PBR) workflow plays a huge part in modern graphics specifically in gaming. Generally, 3D material creation and texture science is a mixture of texture maps and surface properties, as shown in Figure 2-14. With a PBR approach, we can create seamless, more accurate, and super-realistic results easily accepted by game engine renderers. Rendering graphics in games requires a complex algorithm to achieve the best result.

Figure 2-14. *PBR textures*

Using PBR we can minimize the complexity of the algorithm. PBR essentially uses the physical behavior of light to render natural-looking materials, as shown in Figure 2-15, because real-world simulations change with the conditions of light and physics.

Figure 2-15. *Maps for game texturing*

Game Engines

Game engines provide an architecture to game developers for creating and running a game. In general, a game engine is dedicated software for creating games, as shown in Figure 2-16. A game engine provides easy-to-use tools for physics input, real-time rendering, scripting, dynamics, collision detection, artificial intelligence, and more without the need for too much programming from scratch.

We can divide games into two genres.

- **2D games**, e.g., puzzles, platformers, arcade games, racing games, role-playing games, tower defense, adventure games, rogue-likes, fighting games, etc.

- **3D games**, e.g., adventure games, first-person shooters, survival games, virtual reality (VR) games, vehicle simulation, war games, life simulations, etc.

Figure 2-16. *Game engines*

Each game engine has its own strengths and weaknesses. Each has its advantages for certain projects. Also, game engines have their own style and game plan. Unity, Unreal Engine, Corona SDK, Sprite Kit, Marmalade SDK, Construct, Game Maker Studio, and Godot Game Engine are preferred tools by developers and industry experts at this time.

To develop any game, you need to follow these basic steps:

1. Concept phase

2. 2D/3D content creation

3. Level design

4. Lighting

5. Implementation

6. Release

This concludes the brief introduction to the graphics in the game industry. I hope that you now have a good idea about how graphics and game engines work. In the next chapter, we will explore the texturing workflows and pipelines that are currently in use in the industry.

CHAPTER 3

Texturing Workflow

The 3D painting workflow for texturing has become popular because it is intuitive and easy to understand when you are painting your materials. To use it, you'll need several types of texture maps that together make up a material. And with different types of texture maps come different types of texturing workflows. What we are going to focus on in this book is PBR texturing and two of its main types: the metallic-roughness workflow and the specular-glossiness workflow. But before we dive deep into these topics, I'll talk about how texturing works.

3D printing, virtual reality, and modeling are popular nowadays. In all of these technologies, textures and patterns play a vital role. The method used to generate three-dimensional objects in two-dimensional projections is called *UV mapping* and is shown in this chapter. Bitmap textures are made up of pixels that are laid in an integral position (via x, y coordinates) of the UV map. *Texture* can be described as the physical attributes of a surface such as color, bumpiness, roughness, and reflectivity (Figure 3-1 and Figure 3-2).

Figure 3-1. *Texturing workflow*

A. Kumar, *Beginning PBR Texturing*, https://doi.org/10.1007/978-1-4842-5899-6_3

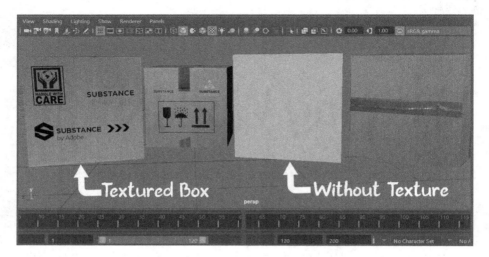

Figure 3-2. *Texturing workflow result*

Game Texturing Pipeline

Let's take a look at the process of creating a game asset. There are 11 steps to creating an entire game asset, as shown in Figure 3-3. Although our main focus is the texturing part here, in later chapters, we will cover everything from step 4 onward.

Here is a quick rundown of the process in brief. Game assets are created in a 3D modeling application; whether they are sculpted or poly modeled is entirely the choice of the artist. A sculpting or high poly detailing process will usually follow the creation process. The sculpted or high poly models are usually not imported into game engines as they will slow down the rapid rendering required for games. Instead, a low poly model is created on which you can bake down the details from the high poly model into normal maps. Baking is usually done in software such as Marmoset Toolbag, Substance Painter/Designer, xNormal, etc. In our case, we will be using Substance Painter. This baking process creates maps such as a curvature map, normal map, AO map, etc., which are further used in the texturing process. After texturing/painting is done, we can export and set up the materials and models in the render/game engine of our choice.

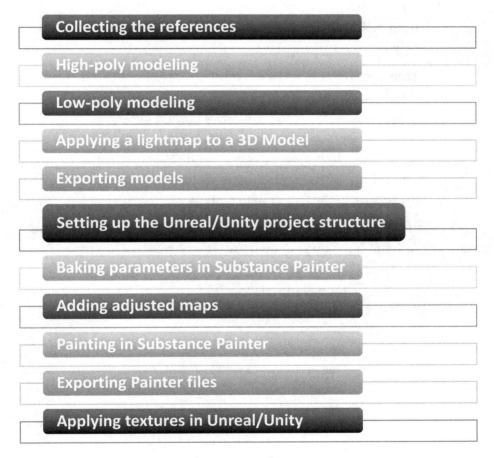

Figure 3-3. *Game asset creation pipeline*

Useful Tips for Texture Artists

Every artist should remember two key points.

- **_References study_**: Before starting the texturing, the artist should study the physical properties of textures from real-life examples and specifically look at how light hits the surface of the model.

- **_Your own library_**: Whenever you are traveling around the globe and find anything interesting, capture the images and save them in your own library. These can be photographs anything such as wood, bricks, fur, clouds, cloth, tiles, etc. Later, with the help of the Photoshop software, you can tweak the images and use the texture for further enhancements.

You can also access the web sites in Figure 3-4 to get 3D material and texture libraries to build up your own texture and material library.

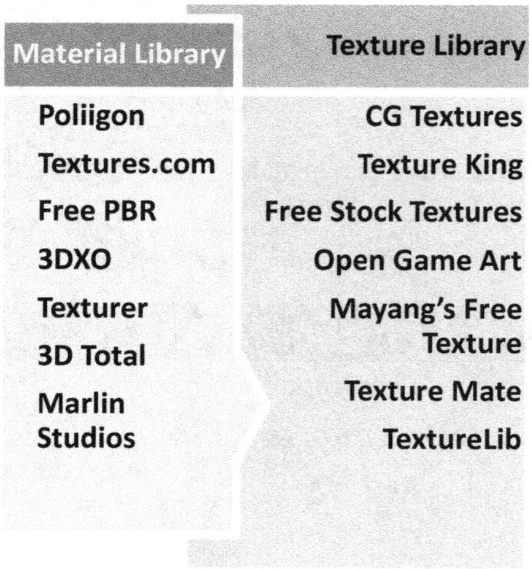

Material Library	Texture Library
Poliigon	CG Textures
Textures.com	Texture King
Free PBR	Free Stock Textures
3DXO	Open Game Art
Texturer	Mayang's Free Texture
3D Total	
Marlin Studios	Texture Mate
	TextureLib

Figure 3-4. *Examples of available 3D material and texture libraries*

What Is UV Mapping?

A *UV map* is a 2D representation constructed from the UV coordinates of the surface of a 3D model, as shown in Figure 3-5. The *U* represents the horizontal axis, and the *V* represents the vertical axis of the 2D space. Each UV has a corresponding point in 3D space called a *vertex*.

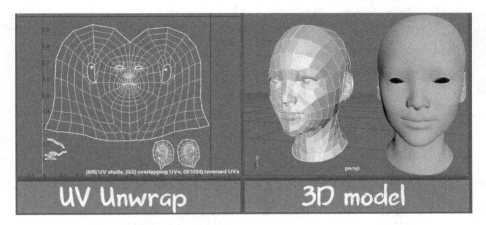

Figure 3-5. *UV unwrapping*

Types of Textures

Texture refers to the immediate tangible feel of a surface and the visual impression of simple stimuli such as color, orientation, and intensity in an image.

There are many types of textures as per the requirements of 3D. When you work in the gaming industry, the following types of maps are essential to generate hyper-realistic results (see Figure 3-6). The types of maps also depend on the game engine or studio workflow.

- Diffuse map

- Albedo map

- Transparency/alpha map

35

- Specular map

- Bump map

- Normal map

- Displacement map

- Ambient occlusion map

The following are more detailed descriptions of the map types:

- **Diffuse**: Diffuse maps represent the overall color of the model; this is the most common type of texture. A bitmap image, captured from a camera, painted, or scanned, can be used as a diffuse map to portray the photorealistic quality of a 3D object. Diffuse has the information of light and shadow.

- **Albedo**: An albedo map is similar to a diffuse map. It has had all the lighting and shadow information removed from it and is literally the color values of the image.

- **Opacity or transparency**: A transparency map depends upon the gray values of an image. Usually the black parts will be opaque, and the white parts will be visible.

- **Specular**: A specular map defines the shininess of the surface at a certain position.

- **Bump**: A bump map is used to create the relief on the surface. We can use a bump map to generate the illusion of depth on the surface of the 3D model. A bump map is generally used to generate virtual scratches, cracks, tiny surface details, etc. The virtual depth depends upon the camera angle. When the value is close to white, the result looks like it is protruding out of the surface, and black tends to push it into the surface. It's not vertex dependent.

- **Normal**: This type of map is used to project high-resolution model details on a low-resolution model. On the basis of chorochromatic map, a normal map texture changes the normal of a pixel.

- **Displacement**: A displacement map is vertex dependent. This map generates physical depth based on the grayscale value of the map.

- **Ambient occlusion**: An ambient occlusion map is used to generate the shadows or darkness caused by the closeness of objects.

Figure 3-6. *Examples of a variety of maps for game texturing*

A few more types of maps are useful for creating the best results in game production pipelines such as ID maps, parallax maps, glossiness maps, vector displacements, height maps, fuzz maps, roughness maps, cavity maps, curvature maps, translucency or thickness maps, etc.

Now you know about the maps, so what maps are most important and commonly used in production? If you using a PBR metallic-roughness workflow, then you will need the albedo, metallic, roughness, normal, and ambient occlusion maps. For a PBR specular-glossiness workflow, you will need the diffuse, specular, glossiness, normal, and ambient occlusion maps. Which workflow you use depends on your engine of choice. The Unity game engine uses the specular-glossiness workflow, while Unreal Engine 4 uses the metallic-roughness workflow. In the next chapter, you will see how texturing works in movies and in games and how they are different from each other.

CHAPTER 4

Texturing Games vs. Texturing Movies

In this chapter, you will see the differences between texturing for games versus texturing for movies.

Texture mapping is the process of assigning the colors to the pixels on a 3D model to simulate four attributes (see Figure 4-1).

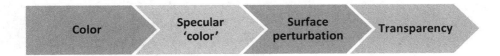

Color   Specular 'color'   Surface perturbation   Transparency

Figure 4-1. *Four attributes simulated by texture mapping*

Texture use in a game should be lower resolution than in films. Texture resolution in a game is usually taken from the number of pixels per meter, whereas in films, the texture resolution and details are per the level of details visible in the camera. Therefore, in a close-up shot, an object's texture in a film may contain hundreds of texture maps. For example, human skin for films ca generate several maps alone for subsurface scattering (SSS) scattering. In games, objects usually have from one to three texture maps. Usually, in games, we use a diffuse map, a specular map, a bump or normal bump, and an alpha map. In a game, we use tillable textures to save memory and also try to create details with many similar objects, so with a single texture, we can optimize the game. However, in films, you would usually avoid using elements repeatedly so

© Abhishek Kumar 2020
A. Kumar, *Beginning PBR Texturing*, https://doi.org/10.1007/978-1-4842-5899-6_4

you can create variation. In a film, we maximum the use of handmade or photo-based textures to generate more realistic results; for game textures nowadays, artists prefer PBR textures. For games currently, there are still some technical limitations to using high-resolution textures, but in the coming year, they will no longer be a barrier; a game engine's texture streaming pipeline will automatically load textures based on several parameters, with the most critical factor being the texture loading based on the distance to the camera.

Texture Pipeline for Movies

To achieve the best result while texturing assets for movies, Figure 4-2 shows the commonly used steps.

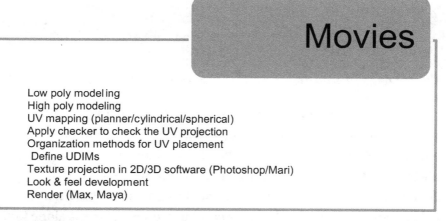

Figure 4-2. *Texturing workflow for movies*

Texture Pipeline for Games

To achieve the best result while texturing assets for movies, Figure 4-3 shows the commonly used steps and the best examples of texturing in games in the media and entertainment industry.

Games

Create high poly model
Retopology
Low poly model
UV projection
Determine the quality needed for the textures
Baking (normal, displacement, ambient occlusion map)
Texturing (dynamic texture, procedural texture)
Export texture
Import to 3D application (Max, Maya) or game engines (Unity, UE4)

Figure 4-3. *Texturing workflow for games*

Common Pipelines and Similarities for Games and Films

The approaches to the modeling and texturing pipeline varies depending on the requirements of the studio. Figure 4-4 shows a few texturing pipeline methods.

Traditional Method

Model in 3D application (Max/Maya)
Unwrap in 3D application (Max/Maya)
Texture in 2D application (Photoshop/Painter)
Add-on application to generate normal/bump map (Crazybump)
Render in 3D application (Max/Maya)

Standard Method

Model in 3D application (Max/Maya)
Unwrap in 3D application (Max/Maya)
Export low poly to sculpting application (Mudbox/Zbrush)
Bake all textures
Render in 3D application

New Generation Method

Sculpt in application (Zbrush/Mudbox)
Retopolize to create low poly
Unwrap the model
Bake texture from high poly to low poly
Render

Figure 4-4. *Examples of texturing pipeline methods*

Note   To put it simply, in movies, we are doing high poly modeling with a high level of detail in texturing to give realistic results. In gaming, we are using a low poly model with a high level of detail in texturing to give better performance results for playing the games.

In next chapter, I will discuss the various traditional and modern texturing methods and their pros and cons. This will help you decide which method is best suited to you.

CHAPTER 5

PBR Texturing vs. Traditional Texturing

In computer graphics, a texture is the digital representation of the appearance of a surface. There are two types of textures.

- 3D textures or procedural textures

- 2D texture or bitmap textures

Procedural texturing is the process of creating a texture that was generated parametrically by using algorithms and a combination of texture maps and masks for generating minor details such as metal, plastic, etc. (see Figure 5-1). It has an infinite level of precision due to seamless texture generation. The drawback of this type of texture is that it lacks human judgment for the accurate placement of effects on textures.

© Abhishek Kumar 2020

A. Kumar, *Beginning PBR Texturing*, https://doi.org/10.1007/978-1-4842-5899-6_5

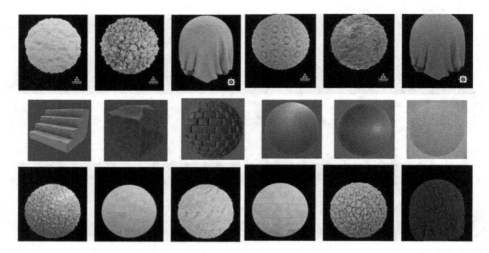

Figure 5-1. *Procedural texturing*

Texturing Using 3D Painting Applications

In the past, textures were also created with photographs and hand-painted bitmaps, but nowadays in the gaming industry textures are usually generated procedurally. There are multiple applications now available to generate procedural textures, such as the Substance tools, Quixel, 3D-Coat, MARI, Armor Paint, Mudbox, and ZBrush (see Figure 5-2).

Figure 5-2. *3D paint applications*

Bitmap texturing or traditional texturing is the simplest and most controllable way of adding texture projection to 3D models. In this methodology, UV unwrapping without overlapping is mandatory. Figure 5-3 shows some examples of bitmap textures.

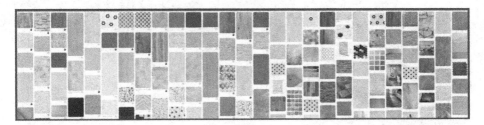

Figure 5-3. *Bitmap textures*

Texturing Using 2D Painting Applications

Besides 3D applications, you can also use 2D painting application to create textures in procedural way. After opening the UV map, you can use Photoshop or Corel Painter to paint the texture map on that UV map. After 2D painting, you will usually connect that bitmap image to the diffuse color and other material/shader nodes as per the requirements. Figure 5-4 shows some 2D painting applications.

Figure 5-4. *2D painting applications*

PBR Textures in the Gaming Industry

The Substance suite and the Quixel suite both have the flexibility to generate any kind of PBR, including physically based, realistic-looking, material, and so on. The artist can then integrate it with any industry-preferred render engine. You can see examples of some images at https://www.substance3d.com/industries/film/ and https://quixel.com/gallery (Figure 5-5).

Figure 5-5. *Artwork produced with Substance*

Figures 5-6. *Artwork produced with Quixel*

I hope you now know the basic differences between PBR texturing and traditional texturing. In the next chapter, I will explore in depth everything that the Substance suite offers so you can get to know more about each application contained in the package.

CHAPTER 6

Substance Suite and Substance Painter

Substance Painter is a real-time 3D texturing and painting application. Substance Painter allows users to create PBR-based textures using hand-painting as well as procedural workflows. It was originally developed for use in films and games, but currently it is widely used in the architecture, product design, and automobile design industries. This application is almost universally used in the video game industry for texturing assets. In addition, several big film studios are also introducing Substance Painter into their pipelines.

Why Substance?

There are several competing software applications in the field of real-time 3D texturing. Software like Mari, the Quixel suite, Quixel Mixer, BodyPaint 3D, ArmorPaint, etc., are some of the most prominent competitors to Substance Painter. Some of them are even free such as ArmorPaint and Quixel Mixer (free for the entire year of 2020). The question is, which software should you pick, and is it worth paying for a premium software

© Abhishek Kumar 2020

A. Kumar, *Beginning PBR Texturing*, https://doi.org/10.1007/978-1-4842-5899-6_6

application when there are free alternatives available? Well, I picked Substance Painter because it is way ahead of all the software, for the following reasons:

- **Procedural workflow**: By far Substance Painter has the strongest procedural workflow. There are hundreds of tools, filters, generators, procedural maps, smart masks, etc., that give Substance Painter a huge advantage.

- **Direct integration with Substance Designer**: Substance Designer is a texture authoring tool that allows users to create complex textures from scratch using mathematical functions and nodes. Once you have created something in Designer, it can be easily exported into Substance Painter for use as a material. Along with all the exposed parameters, you get a huge number of varieties and almost infinite randomized variations of them.

- **Industry standard**: Substance Painter is the industry standard when it comes to texturing for games, architecture, product design, and automobile design. Substance has been widely used in the game industry and is slowly making its way into the film industry as well. So, this is the prime time to learn and master this software.

- **Huge community**: Substance has a large and helpful community on Substance Share that is constantly creating and sharing tools, materials, filters, etc., as shown in Figure 6-1. Artists also create guides and tutorials on YouTube and other web sites. You can also find premium-quality assets and tutorials to buy.

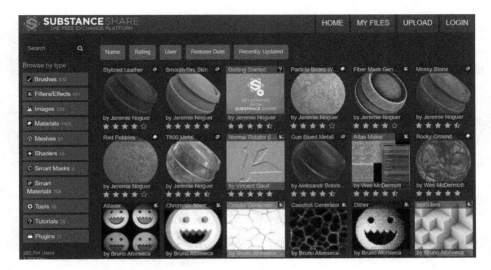

Figure 6-1. *Substance Share has a large library of resources available for free*

Uses of Other Substance Suite Applications

There are four products in the Substance Suite package: Substance Painter, Substance Designer, Substance Alchemist, and access to Substance Source. Each one serves a unique purpose and has a specific role in the texturing pipeline.

Substance Source

Substance Source is a library of premium materials meticulously created by experts using Substance Designer, which gives them a lot of flexibility (Figure 6-2). A Substance subscription comes with 30 credits per month; this allows you to download 30 assets per month, and the credits stack up month after month as long as the subscription is active. Materials can be downloaded and used directly by any other Substance application or product that supports Substance files.

49

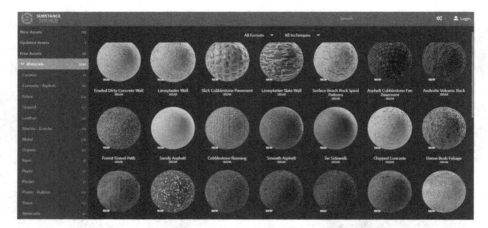

Figure 6-2. *Substance Source is a premium material library*

Substance Source is the most affordable material library simply because it is included in the Substance subscription, and you can absolutely get your money's worth from this entire subscription. If you have a student license of Substance, then you can still download the free materials by clicking the Free Assets section.

Substance Alchemist

Substance Alchemist is a dedicated scan processing and material creation tool that is simpler to use than Designer. With it you can create materials by processing a single image or by processing a multi-angle scan of a surface. Users can also create new materials by merging existing materials and running filters and effects on them. This allows users to create a huge library of materials in a short time.

The left side of the Substance Alchemist (Figure 6-3) contains the shelf where all the resources are stored, and on the top-left side of the screen are modes that you can switch between: Explore, Inspire, Create, and Manage. Figure 6-4 shows an example creation.

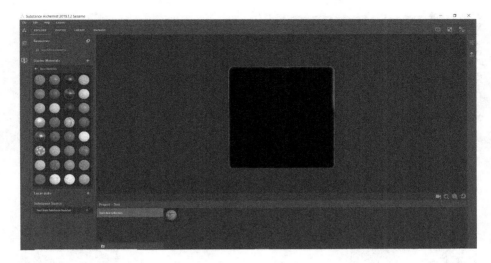

Figure 6-3. *Default UI of Substance Alchemist*

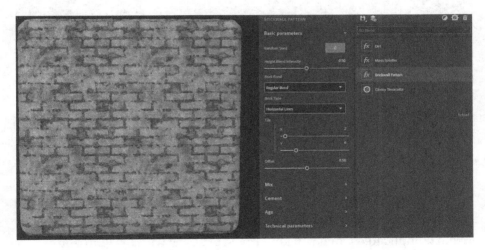

Figure 6-4. *Example of Substance Alchemist creation*

Substance Designer

Substance Designer is a material authoring tool that allows users to create materials from scratch using nodes and mathematical functions (Figure 6-5). This gives users absolute control over what they want to create. Substance Designer is also used to create other tools for Substance Painter such as filters and generators.

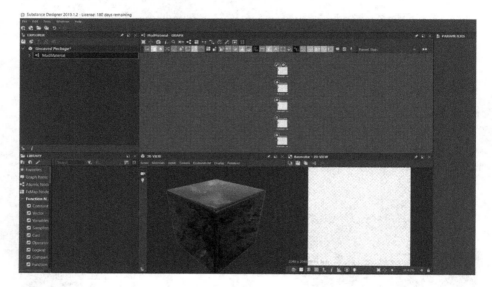

Figure 6-5. *Default UI of Substance Designer*

Substance Designer can create very detailed and realistic materials with the help of nodes. Although the node tree may look daunting at first, it is not all that complicated when you get the gist of how it works (Figure 6-6).

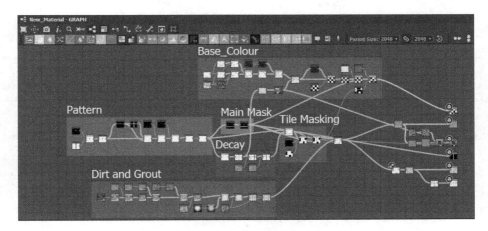

Figure 6-6. *A node tree inside Substance Designer*

This was an introduction to the software available in the Substance Suite package. Next let's see the hardware configuration required to run Substance Painter.

CHAPTER 7

Hardware Specifications for Your Computer

Substance Painter is a 3D painting application with innovative features and workflow improvements to make the creation of textures for 3D game design easier. Users and industry experts alike recommend it as the most user-friendly 3D painter application. For high-quality textures, you need to have a powerful machine to run Substance Painter. In this chapter, let's understand the recommended hardware configuration for a personal computer.

Most 3D software applications require a graphics processing unit (GPU) for better results and fast processing, and your central processing unit (CPU) has to be compatible with your GPU. Only then will you get fast processing. Let's compare the GPU to the CPU.

GPU vs. CPU

If the CPU is the mind of the machine, then the GPU is the heart of a personal computer (Figure 7-1). A CPU is good at handling multiple tasks, but a GPU can handle a few specific tasks very quickly such as rendering, texturing, and playing or creating games. The GPU and CPU both help to render the image, but the methodology involved in computing and rendering the images is different (Table 7-1).

© Abhishek Kumar 2020
A. Kumar, *Beginning PBR Texturing*, https://doi.org/10.1007/978-1-4842-5899-6_7

Figure 7-1. *A GPU card*

Table 7-1. *CPU vs. GPU*

CPU	GPU
Known as the central processing unit	Known as the graphics processing unit
Low latency	High throughput
Good for serial processing	Good for parallel processing
Executes several operations at once	Can do thousands of operations at once

CPUs are built-in and stable, and they utilize cores to process tasks in sequence. A CPU is completely integrated with the computer architecture and produces reliable renders. Therefore, a CPU offers a seamless user experience. GPUs consist of many smaller cores to instruct all their resources to handle the multiple task at once. Based on research, the execution time of a GPU renderer is about 25 to 50 times faster than conventional CPU renderers.

Note   A PBR shader requires heavy computing, so having a good GPU is important. If you have less processing power, you should paint on single channels only.

Recommended Hardware

Figure 7-2 shows the recommended hardware configuration required to run Substance Painter properly.

CPU: Requires a 64-bit processor
Intel i5 or above on it.
AMD Ryzen also a good choice
RAM: 16 GB or above on it.
OS: Windows 7 / 8 / 10   (64-bit mandatory)
Graphic Card: Choose any of the following:

- NVIDIA GeForce GTX 600
- NVIDIA Quadro K2000
- AMD Radeon HD 7000
- AMD Radeon Pro WX-series /
- Pro Duo - AMD FirePro W-series
- FirePro S-series

PIXEL SHADER: 5.0
VERTEX SHADER: 5.0
FREE DISK SPACE: 2 GB

Figure 7-2. *Hardware recommendation*

To perform high-performance computing (HPC), companies have started to use CPUs along with graphics cards to reduce system downtime and to achieve a high-performance result. Nowadays GPUs offer many benefits and are an important part of high-performance computing as they are widely used for computer graphics, AI, computer vision, supercomputing, and deep learning as well as in the healthcare and life sciences industries.

The recommended hardware specifications in Figure 7-2 are required for running the software. If your PC build meets or exceeds these requirements, then you are good to go.

In the next chapter, we will jump right into the Substance Painter and explore its GUI.

CHAPTER 8

Painters' Graphical User Interface

Substance Painter is popular because of its user-friendly viewport and interface. In this chapter, you'll explore its graphical user interface in detail.

The UI and Tools

When you launch Substance Painter, you are greeted by the welcome screen, as shown in Figure 8-1.

Figure 8-1. *Graphical user interface of Substance Painter*

© Abhishek Kumar 2020

A. Kumar, *Beginning PBR Texturing*, https://doi.org/10.1007/978-1-4842-5899-6_8

In this window, you can choose to go to the official pages including the tutorials, documentation, or forums. Alternatively, you can also go to the Substance Share page to download community-created brushes, materials, tools, filters, etc., for free.

You can simply click the Close button to close this window. However, if you are a beginner and if you do not have a model prepared for texturing, then you can click the Start Painting button to open a Meet Mat example scene, which gives you a UV unwrapped 3D model so that you can play around with tools and brushes.

The interface of Substance Painter is highly customizable; it allows you to move around and dock all the shelves wherever you want based on your preferences. So, unless you have changed anything, you should see the default layout of the Substance Painter interface. If the layout has been modified, you can click Windows and choose Reset Layout from the drop-down menu to get back to the default layout.

Located at the top of the screen is the menu bar, which houses the basic function menus such as the File menu, Edit menu, etc.

Just below the menu bar in the left corner of the screen is the toolbar/Tool menu. This contains all the tools that you will require while painting or texturing, such as the Brush tool and the Eraser tool.

At the bottom of the screen is the Shelf. This contains all the materials, brushes, smart masks, materials, procedurals, etc. These are the assets required for texturing an object both manually as well as procedurally.

On the right side of the screen, you will find four windows docked together: Texture Set List, Layer Stack, Texture Set Settings, and Properties. The Texture Set List window contains a list of texture sets that are automatically generated based on the number of material IDs present in an imported mesh. One texture set is generated for each material ID. Figure 8-2 shows the Texture Set List window.

Figure 8-2. *Texture Set List window*

The Texture Set Settings window (see Figure 8-3) allows you to modify various parameters of each individual texture set (e.g., their resolution) as well as manage the mesh maps present in it. New texture channels can be added or removed based on the requirements in this menu.

Figure 8-3. *Texture Set Settings window*

The Layer Stack window (see Figure 8-4) allows you to create, edit, and manage layers individually for each texture set. You can change blending modes and various other parameters based on your needs. A layer in Substance Painter stores all the manually painted details and procedural effects used for texturing a mesh.

Figure 8-4. *Layers window*

The Properties window (see Figure 8-5) contains all the parameters related to layers, brushes, materials, etc., that can be modified to achieve the desired result. This window can also be accessed by right-clicking the viewport.

Figure 8-5. *Properties window*

The viewport settings (see Figure 8-6) are located at the top-right corner of the screen just below the toolbar.

Figure 8-6. *Viewport settings*

These settings allow you to change how your model is displayed and also allow you to paint in all the different views. If you click the drop-down menu, you will see a list of different material and channel views categorized into three categories: Lighting, Single channel, and Mesh maps. Material under Lighting is the default view in which you will work. The Single channel and Mesh map categories will disable lighting and isolate and display the selected map as used in the 3D mesh. Figure 8-7 shows an example of a normal map being displayed in a project.

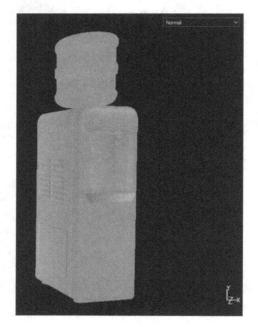

Figure 8-7. *The normal map displayed in Single-channel mode*

Two significant types of viewports are 2D viewports and 3D viewports. The 2D viewport displays the UV layout of the mesh loaded in the painter, while the 3D viewport shows the 3D model. One can directly paint in both views, and changes are applied universally to the model. It is subjective when one viewport is useful over another, but mostly the texturing work is done in 3D viewport because you can see all the angles of your model and the environment's lighting. Figure 8-8 shows an example; the left side of the screen is a 3D viewport, while the right side is a 2D viewport.

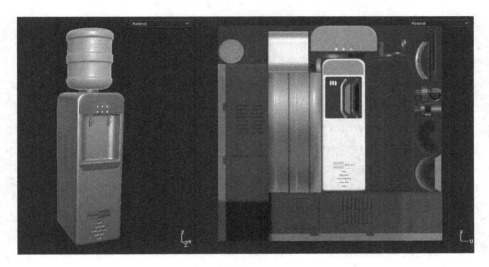

Figure 8-8. *Split-screen view displaying both 2D and 3D aspects*

At the top-right side of the screen, you can find four buttons that are collapsed windows, namely, Display settings ⬚, Shader settings ⬚, History ⬚, and Logs ⬚. You can click the respective button to open the menus.

The display settings are used to globally control the look and feel of a project by modifying usually parameters of three submenus, which are environment, camera, and viewport.

Shader settings are used to change the shader type that you want to use or modify the various parameters of the currently active shader.

History stores all your paint strokes, modifications, etc. It basically allows you to store anything that you do while texturing or painting a 3D scene.

The log is where Substance Painter displays technical information such as warnings and errors for you to see.

Guide to the Shelf

Now we will take a detailed look at the resource/asset shelf. This window is located at the bottom of the screen and is named simply Shelf. Substance Painter ships with lots of default resources that you can use for your texturing/painting work. Any additional resources required can be obtained from either Substance Share, a community-based resource sharing platform, or Substance Source, a curated premium-quality resource platform managed by Allegorithmic that provides materials at fair prices.

As for these resources, they are categorized into various categories that you can see on the left side of the Shelf window. The categories work as filters for sorting assets and make it easier for users to find what they need. When you click a category, then only the assets that fall under that category are displayed. Alternatively, you can use the search bar at the top of the Shelf window (see Figure 8-9) to define a custom filter or search anything by name.

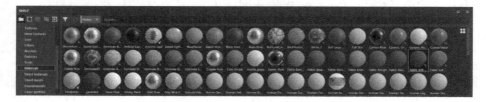

Figure 8-9. *Shelf in Substance Painter*

Now let's discuss the most important and commonly used categories in brief in the order they are present in Painter.

- **Project**: This category displays mesh maps generated during the baking process.

- **Alphas**: These are black-and-white or grayscale images that are generally used to create custom brushes and stamps.

- **Grunges**: These are grayscale images that are used to generate imperfections or simply alter how a material looks.

- **Procedurals**: This tab contains procedural noises and patterns that are used to alter the look of the material.

- **Textures**: This category contains all the textures that you imported into Substance Painter as well as baked mesh maps.

- **Hard Surfaces**: This category contains normal map stamps that are used to paint normal map information on a mesh.

- **Filters**: This contains effects that can be applied on a layer or a mask to modify it in various procedural ways.

- **Brushes**: This contains custom-made presets for brushes that can be used for painting.

- **Particles**: These are special types of brushes that create paint effects using particles and physics simulation.

- **Tools**: These are types of presets that store both material and brush properties, allowing users to create things such as nails, damages, etc.

- **Materials**: These are created in Substance Designer and are used to define the look and feel of the surface of a model. For example, if you are making a table, then with the help of materials, you can define whether the table will be wood, metal, or glass.

- **Smart Materials**: These are material presets created inside Substance Painter by combining stacks of layers, masks, and effects that can automatically change and adapt according to the 3D mesh on which it is applied.

- **Smart Masks**: These are premade masks and adaptive masks that will automatically adjust according to the 3D model on which it is applied.

- **Environments**: This category contains HDRI light environments that are used for lighting the scene on which you are working. This is for visualizing only and does not affect texturing in any way but will alter the way things look depending on the lighting.

- **Color Profiles**: This category contains color lookup tables (LUTs) that can be used to change how the scene looks, kind of like applying filters on a camera. This is for visualizing as well and does not affect texturing either. See Figure 8-10.

Figure 8-10.   *Color profile with sepia LUTs*

Note   Try to remember all the shortcuts for the painter. It makes your work faster. Use the Windows menu bar and click Settings; then go to the Shortcuts tab, where you get all the information about the shortcuts. Here you can change the shortcuts if you'd like. Also, we are going to talk a lot more about the settings in Chapter 9. Figure 8-11 shows the Settings menu of Substance Painter.

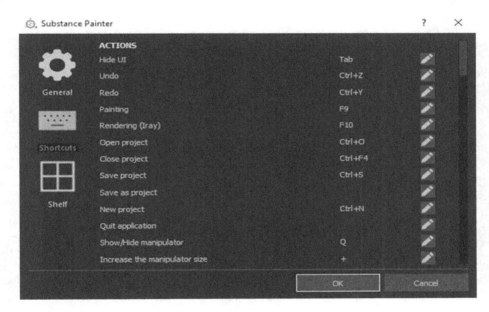

Figure 8-11. *Substance Painter settings*

You are now familiar with the GUI of Substance Painter. In the next chapter, you will see how you can navigate around the viewport of Substance Painter.

CHAPTER 9

Viewport Navigation in Painter

In this chapter, you'll learn about navigating the viewport in Substance Painter.

Keyboard Shortcuts

To navigate Substance Painter smoothly, you need to know some shortcut keys and key combinations, as listed here. LMB means left mouse button, RMB means right mouse button, and MMB means middle mouse button.

Basic Navigation	
Alt+LMB	Rotates view
Alt+MMB	Pans view
Alt+RMB	Zooms view
MMB scroll	Zooms view
Shift+Alt+LMB	Snaps camera according to mouse
F	Centers entire object

(continued)

© Abhishek Kumar 2020
A. Kumar, *Beginning PBR Texturing*, https://doi.org/10.1007/978-1-4842-5899-6_9

Viewport Settings

F1	2D/3D split view
F2	3D-only view
F3	2D-only view
F4	Toggles between 2D and 3D views
F5	Perspective view
F6	Orthographic view
F9	Switches to Painting mode
F10	Switches to Rendering mode
Shift+RMB	Rotates scene HDRI environment
C	Switches between single-channel views
B	Switches between mesh map views
M	Switches to material view

Tool Selection

P	Color picker tool
1	Paint tool
2	Eraser tool
3	Projection tool
4	Polygon Fill tool
5	Smudge tool
6	Clone tool

(continued)

Tool Settings

LMB	Uses active tool/brush
[/]	Decreases/increases brush size
Shift+LMB	Draws straight line between 2 points
Ctrl+Shift+LMB	Draws straight line with 15° snap rotation
S+MMB	Moves/translates stencil
S+LMB	Rotates stencil
S+RMB	Zooms/scales stencil
Shift+S+LMB	Rotates stencil while snapping

Functionality Shortcuts

Ctrl+C	Copies highlighted layer
Ctrl+V	Pastes copied layer
Ctrl+X	Cuts highlighted layer
Ctrl+G	Groups selected layer(s)
Ctrl+D	Duplicates selected layer(s)
Delete	Deletes selected layer(s)

These are the most commonly used shortcuts that are highly recommended. Although they're not mandatory as you can perform most of the actions without having to use shortcuts, remembering these will make your workflow faster. And once you have started using Painter regularly, then everything will become muscle memory, so it is important to practice daily.

Guide to Commonly Used Tools

While painting or texturing anything, you will usually use the Brush tool and Eraser tool the most followed by the Polygon Fill and Projection tool. And on some rare occasions, you might use the Smudge tool and the Clone tool. In this section, I will discuss the Paint tool, Eraser tool, Projection tool, and Polygon Fill tool.

- **Paint tool**: This is the most basic and commonly used tool in Substance Painter. It is basic yet can perform complex tasks, and it is important to have a strong understanding of this tool. This tool can be used to freehand draw, stamp details using alpha/normal maps, use particle effects to dynamically paint details, etc. The possibilities are limited only by your creativity.

- **Eraser tool**: This tool is precisely what the name suggests; it removes painted details from a mesh. All kinds of alphas and particles can be used with the Eraser tool.

- **Projection tool**: This tool is used to project a 2D image onto a 3D surface from the point of view of the camera (Figure 9-1).

Figure 9-1. *Projection tool at work*

- **Polygon Fill tool**: When this tool is active, the paint effect/mask is applied only to the triangle/polygon/ mesh on which you click/select depending on the settings.

Finally, two more tools are used on rare occasions: the Smudge tool and the Clone Stamp tool.

- **Smudge tool**: This tool is used to soften a painted or textured detail or mix/spread information (Figure 9-2).

- **Clone tool**: This tool is used to copy part of the paint or texture from one part of a mesh to another part.

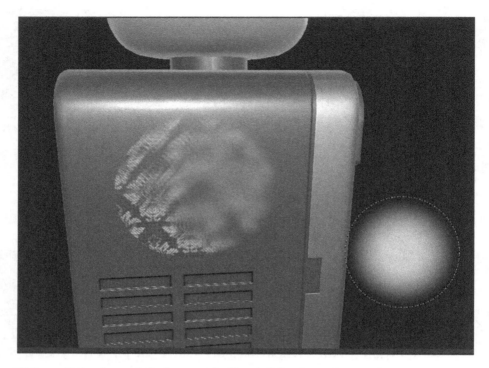

Figure 9-2. *A straightforward effect of the Smudge tool*

So, now you know how to navigate the viewport of Substance Painter. In the next chapter, you will learn how you can set up your project.

CHAPTER 10

Setting Up a Project

To start painting, you need a 3D model. The 3D model should be in OBJ, FBX, or ABC format. Those are the only files you can import into Substance Painter. You may have your own model; if not, you can download one from the Internet to practice on.

Getting Started with Substance Painter

First launch Substance Painter. Then you need to select File ➤ New. Once you do that, you will be greeted by the "New project" window (Figure 10-1). Right now the OK button should be grayed out, or deactivated, because first you need to import a model.

© Abhishek Kumar 2020
A. Kumar, *Beginning PBR Texturing*, https://doi.org/10.1007/978-1-4842-5899-6_10

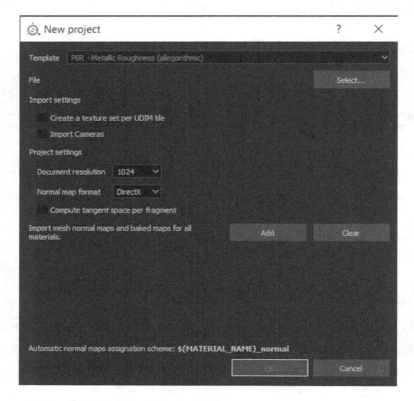

Figure 10-1. *"New project" window*

To import a model, you need to click the Select button to open the file browser and from there navigate to the 3D mesh you want to open. Click Open to load it into Substance Painter. Once the model has been loaded, it should appear next to the File title (Figure 10-2).

Figure 10-2. *Selected file's location being displayed*

Now the OK button should be active, so click it to initialize the project. Once done, you should see your model sitting in the center of the screen without any textures.

Project Configuration in Detail

Before we continue, let's discuss more about this "New project" window. You have probably seen there are few settings in the "New project" window. We will explore them now. First, you need to know what your target render engine is.

Templates: Different engines use different types of maps for rendering. Some may use the specular-gloss workflow, while others may use the metallic-roughness workflow. Also, the normal map format may differ as some engines prefer OpenGL while others use DirectX. For this purpose, various templates have been preset inside Substance Painter that automatically set up your project correctly. The presets also allow you to export maps in a way that is suitable for your preferred render engine.

Import settings: This heading contains two checkboxes under it.

- **Create a texture set per UDIM tile**: This will create a new texture set for every UDIM tile contained in your model if it has any.

- **Import Cameras**: This will import cameras in the present file from your exported scene, which you can switch between any time by pressing the arrow keys on your keyboard.

Project settings: This section has three settings.

- **Document resolution**: This allows you to change the resolution of your texture square. Substance Painter uses a nondestructive workflow, so you can start your project with any resolution and change it later without any problems. Substance Painter will simply recalculate all the maps.

79

- **Normal map format**: This allows you to choose between the OpenGL and DirectX normal map formats. Different render engines will use either of the maps, and you should choose your map accordingly.

- **Compute tangent space per fragment**: If this checkbox is enabled, then normals, binormals, and tangents for the imported mesh are calculated in Pixel Shader. It's best to keep this unchecked most of the time unless you want to export your maps to Unreal Engine.

The last option is "Import mesh normal maps and baked maps for all materials," which you can use to import any mesh maps like the normal map that you baked outside of Substance Painter and imported into Painter.

In the next chapter, you will see what mesh maps are and how to bake them.

CHAPTER 11

Baking and the Importance of Mesh Maps

In this chapter, I will discuss what mesh maps are, their importance, and how to create them. The first thing that you should do after importing a 3D mesh into Substance Painter is to bake mesh maps. This can be done by going to the Texture Set Settings window and clicking the Bake Mesh Maps button (see Figure 11-1). Alternatively, you can go to Edit menu and select Bake Mesh Map, or you can use the shortcut Ctrl+Shift+B.

© Abhishek Kumar 2020
A. Kumar, *Beginning PBR Texturing*, https://doi.org/10.1007/978-1-4842-5899-6_11

Figure 11-1. Bake Mesh Maps button

Introduction to the Baker

Baking refers to the action of transferring mesh onto textures. This information is then read by shaders and substance filters to perform advanced effects. Once you click it, the Baker window will open, as shown in Figure 11-2.

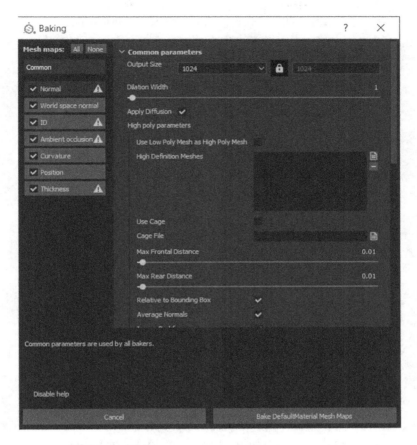

Figure 11-2. *Baking window*

As you can see, there are a lot of settings in this window, which may look overwhelming at first. But you will usually modify only a few essential ones. The window has been split into three panels; the right side is the Parameters window that you can adjust to change how textures are baked. The left side contains various bakers that will bake the corresponding maps. The third at the bottom displays the help message for each baker. By default, the common parameters are displayed, but you can click the individual bakers to display the settings related to them.

- **Output Size**: This setting changes the resolution of the texture square used for store-baked information. Usually, its value depends on the texture size of the asset, but most commonly 2048 and 4096 are used.

- **Use Low Poly Mesh as High Poly Mesh**: Select this option if you don't have a high poly mesh. The high poly mesh is used to bake high-quality details present in the high poly version of the model into a low poly version of the same model. It is not mandatory and is usually not used for smaller assets, but it is recommended if the model is larger and needs to have more details.

- **High Definition Meshes**: Use the file icon next to the empty space to load high poly meshes, which will be used to bake highly detailed maps.

- **Use Cage**: Select this option if you need to use a caged file for baking purposes.

- **Max Frontal/Rear Distance sliders**: These sliders are used to control how far the rays will be cast from. These settings depend on how big your model is or how many tiny details are there.

- **Antialiasing**: This setting controls the antialiasing method for your textures. The higher the value, the crisper the detail will be in smaller areas of your texture. High values will also increase the baking time by a pretty big margin.

- **Match**: This setting determines what method is used while matching a low poly mesh to its corresponding high poly mesh. The naming of each part of a mesh has to be done inside the 3D software. The name of a low poly part of a mesh must correspond to its high poly counterpart. For example, for a bed, there can be Mattress_low and Mattress_high.

- **Self Occlusion**: Now if you click the Ambient Occlusion and Thickness tabs, you will see additional settings. But here we are interested in one setting called Self Occlusion. This is similar to the Match option of Common Parameters window. That means the baker matches geometries by their mesh names.

Uses of Mesh Maps

The mesh maps are the surface details of a 3D mesh transferred to a 2D texture; mesh maps serve several purposes. Normal and ambient occlusion maps are used to transfer details from high-resolution meshes to low-resolution meshes as well as generate procedural effects based on their data. Curvature, thickness, and position maps are exclusively used to generate different kinds of procedural effects on the mesh by using smart masks, smart materials, etc.

These are best understood with the practical examples that you will see in the upcoming chapters. But for now, I will give you a general overview of them.

- **Normal map**: Normal maps are used to fake lighting information of high-resolution details on a low-resolution mesh without having to add more geometry to it. Not only that, Substance Painter uses this type of map to generate procedural information for the high-resolution data. See Figure 11-3.

Figure 11-3. *Normal map faking geometry information in a low poly mesh*

- **World space normal**: This is another type of normal map that stores the normal coordinates of an object with respect to world space direction. This requires the model to always be static because any kind of movement will cause deformation and warping in displaying the normal maps.

- **ID map**: This map stores the vertex colors that define which part of the model belongs to which material. Every region of a model is given a different ID color, and when imported into Substance Painter, this allows the texturing process to speed up because you can simply choose an ID to quickly apply a material to all those regions.

- **Ambient occlusion map**: This map creates soft shadows and contact shadows on a mesh to simulate the effect of an indirect light source. This effect, although subtle, adds a lot of realism to an object. See Figure 11-4.

Figure 11-4. *The left image has no ambient occlusion, while the right image has ambient occlusion*

- **Curvature map**: This is a grayscale map that stores and represents the concave and convex areas of a mesh. This map is generally used to generate procedural information such as damage and wear.

- **Position map**: This map stores the 3D coordinates of every point of a mesh into its respective texture pixel in the UV. This allows the user to procedurally apply effects that are position-dependent such as dirt collecting on top of objects, moss growing from the bottom of an object, etc.

- **Thickness map**: This is a grayscale map that defines how thick or thin different areas of a mesh are. The darker areas represent thinner parts of a model mesh, while white represents thicker parts of a model. This is commonly used to create a subsurface scattering (SSS) effect.

It is not always necessary to bake all the maps. Bake only the ones you require for your project, which might save you some time. In the next chapter, you will start working with layers and masks.

CHAPTER 12

Working with Materials, Layers, and Masks

Substance Painter has a powerful procedural workflow assisted by various materials, tools, masks, automatic functions, etc. In this chapter, I will discuss materials and smart materials and how you can use them to rapidly texture almost anything. Then I'll discuss layers and masks.

Materials and Smart Materials

Materials are created inside Substance Designer and have lots of exposed parameters (depending on the creator's choices) that allow users to tweak the material according to their needs. They can be either acquired in ready-made form from various sources or created from scratch inside Substance Designer. Substance Source and Gametextures. com are two really great places to get premium ready-made materials for a fair price. As for free resources, there is Substance Share, where members of the Substance community create and share materials and other resources for free.

© Abhishek Kumar 2020
A. Kumar, *Beginning PBR Texturing*, https://doi.org/10.1007/978-1-4842-5899-6_12

Now let's talk about smart materials. These are presets of layers and effects stacked in a way that creates a procedural material that automatically adapts itself according to the topology of the mesh it is applied to. Using them is also easy; just drag and drop them anywhere in your layer stack. Smart materials, once created, will work with any model and can be easily shared across multiple projects and computers. Substance Painter by default ships with more than 100 smart materials that you can further tweak to your liking, and more of them can be acquired from Substance Source.

When texturing an asset in Substance Painter, you need to integrate all the workflows to achieve the result that you want.

Smart materials can be added in two ways.

- By dragging and dropping smart materials from the Shelf into the layer stack

- By clicking the Smart Material button to open a mini-shelf

Once you have made your own material, you can simply save this preset in your Shelf by right-clicking your final layer and clicking Create Smart Material.

Layers and Masks

Layers store all the paint and procedural data in them in their respective channels. Users can decide which channels they want to activate or deactivate. The hierarchy of the layer stack goes from the bottom to the top. The layer at the top is the last layer and gets first priority in rendering, and the layer at the bottom of the stack is considered the first layer and is rendered last. You can enable or disable any layer by clicking the eye icon next to it. Disabling a layer will hide all the information stored in it.

Different types of layers store different types of information. There are three types of layer.

- **Paint layer**: This layer stores any kind of brush strokes or paint information that the user provides.

- **Fill layer**: This layer prevents users from manually painting any kind of information; rather, this has empty channels where users can define what they want to fill.

- **Folders**: These are containers in which you can store multiple layers to better organize everything. or you can say it's a group of the layers. These have all the types of operations available for them that are available for layers.

Layer Operations

Now let's look at the operations that we can perform directly on layers. If you look at the Layers window (see Figure 12-1), you can see that there are a variety of options available that change the behavior of the layers.

Figure 12-1. *Layer operations*

- **Enable/Disable Layers**: This is the most basic operation that allows users to simply enable or disable a layer. This can be done by clicking the eye icon on the left side of the layer. See Figure 12-2.

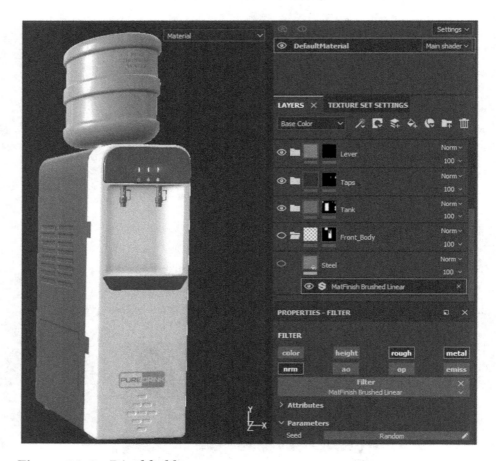

Figure 12-2. *Disabled layers*

- **Change Channel**: You can change the active channel in the layer stack by selecting your desired channel from the drop-down menu at the top-left corner. By default the Base Color channel is selected.

- **Change Blending Mode**: Different blending modes change how differently the layers interact with the layers below it. You can change this behavior by clicking the drop-down menu on the top-right side of every layer. This menu is context-sensitive.

- **Change Opacity**: The opacity of every individual channel of each layer can be changed by using the slider at the bottom right of every layer. This slider is also context sensitive, meaning that it will work only on the currently active channel selected via the Channel drop-down menu.

- **Group Layers**: You can group layers together to make your layer stack clean and organized. This can be done by selecting desired layers by Ctrl+clicking them and then pressing Ctrl+G. Alternatively, you can click the icon shown in Figure 12-3 to create a new folder and drag and drop the layers that you want inside it.

Figure 12-3. *Adding a folder*

There are several other options available in the top-right corner of the Layers window, as you can see in Figure 12-3. The first option from the left is the Add Effects drop-down menu that contains various procedural effects such as Filter, Generator, Anchor Point, etc. These are used to modify the contents inside the layer, so we will discuss them later in the chapter. The second option from the left is Add Mask, which we will discuss next. The next two options are Add (Paint) Layer and Add Fill Layer, respectively, and as their names suggest, these are used to add new layers. The final three options are Add Smart Material, Add Folder, and Delete Layer, respectively.

Masks

Masking allows you to choose where you want certain effects/paint/ material to apply and where not. A black mask removes data from an area, while a white mask keeps data. To add a mask, you need to right-click a layer and then select either "Add black mask" or "Add white mask" depending on the need and convenience. This can be understood with the example cube in Figure 12-4.

Figure 12-4. *Example cube*

Let's say that in the example cube in Figure 12-4 you want the brick material to be applied only on the front face of the cube. Then you can proceed by right-clicking the layer that holds the material and selecting "Add black mask." See Figure 12-5.

Figure 12-5. *Adding a black mask*

Once you have added the mask, then you will see that the entire material disappears. And a mask container appears in the layer in which you added the mask (see Figure 12-6).

Figure 12-6. *Mask container*

The material disappears because the black color in a mask in Substance Painter means the subtraction of everything present in that layer. Now choose the Polygon Fill tool from the Tool window, first from the side toolbar and then from the top toolbar, as shown in Figure 12-7.

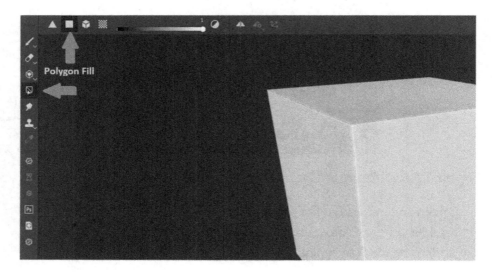

Figure 12-7. Polygon Fill tool

Now make sure that the fill color is set to completely white in the Properties window. See Figure 12-8.

Figure 12-8. Color selection

Finally, your pointer is ready to select faces that you want to be textured with that material. All you have to do is click individual faces or click and drag to draw a box selection. Now, there are several other options available for the Polygon Fill tool, four to be precise. You can see them in Figure 12-7 and Figure 12-8. You can choose your fill method from either of the windows. The first one is the triangle fill, which will fill only triangles. The second one is a polygon fill, which we used already. This tool fills entire quads. The third one is a mesh fill, which will fill the entire mesh or all connected faces to the selected face. The last option is a UV chunk fill, which will simply fill an entire UV island, meaning all the faces that are connected by the same island.

Note   The Polygon Fill tool is basically a black-and-white mask that you can also paint and erase according to your requirements.

Smart Masks

These are special types of mask presets that have special effects when applied to a mesh. The best way to get to know them is to experiment with them as there are about 60 of them and each has a different effect that is described by their name. These are generally used to create dust, damage, moss, rust, etc. Using them is simple; all you have to do is add a black mask and then drag and drop the desired smart mask from the Shelf to the empty black mask. See Figure 12-9 for a simple example.

Figure 12-9. *An example of a smart mask*

If you select the mask container of a smart mask, then you will see that it contains several effects, generators, filters, etc., stacked together. There are several presets available but you can also create them yourself once you have a mask. The smart masks are a way to save a mask and its effect to easily reuse them on other layers or other projects. All you need to do is right-click your mask container and then click the "Create smart mask" option. After that, your smart mask should appear in the Shelf in the "Smart masks" category.

Mask Operations

You can edit masks by using all kinds of tools and effects and even stack them together to create more complex effects.

- **Polygon Fill tool**: This is the most basic and most common way to do masking, as described earlier. When large chunks of parts of a mesh have to be masked, then this method is used as it is a fast way to do it. Once a mask has been added, then you can simply activate the Polygon Fill tool and choose the preferred fill type. After that, simply select the face/mesh that needs to be masked, and that's it.

- **Mask with an ID map**: Masking can be done with the help of an ID map as well. The ID map must be created inside the 3D application by assigning different color IDs to different parts of the 3D mesh based on your design needs. Then you export the map into Substance Painter. ID maps are then created by baking the vertex colors of the mesh into a texture map. Now to create a mask, right-click the layer that needs to be masked and then choose the "Add mask with color selection" option. Then drag and drop the ID map from the Textures category to where it says "Missing ID map" in the Properties window. See Figure 12-10.

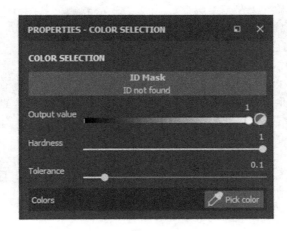

Figure 12-10. *Color Selection properties*

Then use the "Pick a color" option to choose the color you want to be used to mask out.

- **Mask with the Paintbrush tool**: You can also use a custom brush to paint directly on the mask with a grayscale or black-or-white value. In Figure 12-11, I used a square brush to mask the metal and plastic parts of the filter by manually painting in the mask along with the detail created by the normal map.

Figure 12-11. *Masking with the Brush tool*

To keep everything clean and organized, it is advisable to create paint effects on masks, which creates a layer-like system that makes working and error correction easy. This can be done by right-clicking the mask and choosing "Add paint." See Figure 12-12.

Figure 12-12. *Adding a paint effect to a layer*

- **Masking with the Fill effect**: You can use various grunge maps or textures that you created/imported to create a custom mask as well. Simply right-click your mask and choose "Add fill," and it should appear underneath your mask, as shown in Figure 12-13.

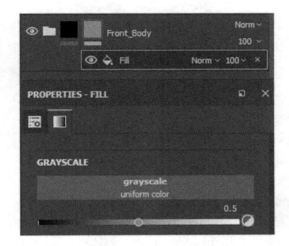

Figure 12-13. *Fill effect under mask*

In the Properties window, you can see that by default Substance fills the Fill effect with a solid grayscale image with a 0.5 value. You can now drag and drop grunge maps or other grayscale textures into channel slots and modify the mask. See Figure 12-14.

Figure 12-14. *An example of a fill mask*

- **Effects of generators and filters on masks**: Generators and filters are applied to further modify the results produced by the mask or in the case of generators to introduce modifications in the first place. Generators are always applied on masks, and we will discuss more about them as well as filters in later chapters.

- **Modifying masks with levels**: You can add levels to your mask by right-clicking a mask container and clicking "Add levels." See Figure 12-15.

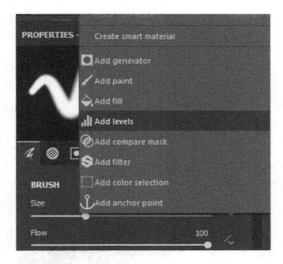

Figure 12-15. *Adding levels*

This option can be used to modify your mask by clamping values or by directly inverting your mask. See Figure 12-16.

Figure 12-16. *Inverting a mask with levels*

You should now be clear on layers, masks, and generators. You'll need to practice using them in order to master them. In the next chapter, I will be discuss how to work with procedurals.

CHAPTER 13

Working with Procedural Maps

In this chapter, you will explore the various procedural tools available in Substance Painter. You will learn about everything you can do with filters and generators and how to create procedural effects automatically using the superior algorithms of Substance Painter. The procedural effects allow you to create complex effects without manual intervention. After that, you will see how you can use various grunge and pattern maps to add further details to your assets.

Filters

You can add filters to either layers or masks to modify their contents. Substance Painter ships with a huge variety of filters that can be used for multiple purposes, and you can acquire even more filters from Substance Share. Filters are created inside Substance Designer.

Depending on the filter type, a filter effect has to be created on the content or on the mask of a layer.

Applying a Filter

There are two ways to apply a filter; which one you use depends on how you intend your filter to work.

© Abhishek Kumar 2020
A. Kumar, *Beginning PBR Texturing*, https://doi.org/10.1007/978-1-4842-5899-6_13

Manually Applying a Filter

The first method of adding a filter to a layer or mask is to right-click and select "Add filter," as shown in Figure 13-1.

Figure 13-1. *Selecting "Add filter"*

Then you will see that a sublayer has been added with the "Filter (empty)" name underneath the layer, and if you select it, its properties will appear in the Properties window. Your Properties window should appear similar to Figure 13-2 depending on the number of texture channels you have added to your project.

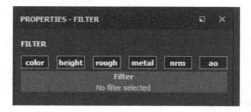

Figure 13-2. *Filter properties*

You can activate/deactivate the channels of your choice to change which channels will be affected by the filter. Now click "No filter selected" and choose MatFinish Rough. As soon as you do that, you'll see the Properties window change, as shown in Figure 13-3.

Figure 13-3. *Filter parameters*

Dragging and Dropping a Filter

The second way to add a filter is to drag a filter from the Filters section of the Shelf and drop it onto a layer, as shown in Figure 13-4.

Figure 13-4. Filters are stored in the Shelf

The effect of each filter varies depending on whether it is applied on a layer or on a mask. Some filters may be incompatible with one or the other.

Commonly Used Filters

Let's explore some commonly used filters and see how they work.

MatFinish Filters

The MatFinish filters are used to create subtle surface imperfections or details on materials. There are nine variations of this filter, with each one creating different types of detail. These filters work on the normal map of the mesh and add procedural grunge maps on them to achieve their effect.

The one I most commonly use is MatFinish Rough to add imperfections to the materials that ship with Substance Painter, as shown in Figure 13-5.

Figure 13-5. *Example of MatFinish Rough*

Another common MatFinish filter is MatFinish Brushed Linear. This creates a procedural brushed effect on the materials. It's useful for adding details to plain materials, as shown in Figure 13-6.

Figure 13-6. *Example of MatFinish Brushed Linear*

These MatFinish filters are applied directly to paint/fill layers, and they work on the normal map channel of the layers.

Blur

The Blur filter is used to soften the pixels of a layer or the result of the effect stack on which it is applied. The Blur filter can be applied to both layers and masks, and the results produced are similar. It can be added to a layer or mask in the same way as any other filter. Once a Blur filter has been applied, its value can be controlled using the slider present in the Properties window.

There are three types of Blur filter available: Blur, Directional Blur, and Slope Blur. Directional Blur and Slope Blur have more advanced but limited uses, so you can experiment with which one suits your needs, but most commonly you will find yourself using Blur as it can easily create the effect you need, as shown in Figure 13-7.

110

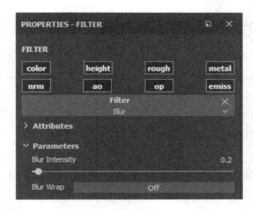

Figure 13-7. *Blur filter properties*

In Figure 13-8, you can see how the Blur filter softens the effect of the MatFinish Brushed Linear. (For comparison, you can compare this to Figure 13-6 where MatFinish Brushed Linear is applied in its unaltered form.)

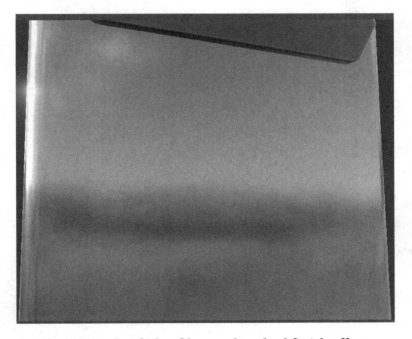

Figure 13-8. *Example of Blur filter on brushed finish effect*

Sharpen

The Sharpen filter sharpens the pixels of the layer/effect stack on which it is applied. It can be applied to both layers and masks for enhancing certain subtle details. You can see in Figure 13-9 how the Sharpen filter exaggerates the subtle lines created by MatFinish Brushed Linear and makes them more apparent.

Figure 13-9. *Example effect of the Sharpen filter*

HSL Perceptive

The HSL Perceptive filter allows you to modify the Hue, Saturation, and Lightness (HSL) values of a material. Once you have created a complex material spanning multiple layers that control its appearance, it becomes really challenging to make an overall color change to it. That's where HSL Perceptive comes in. You can modify the color using this filter by editing its parameters in the Properties window, as shown in Figure 13-10.

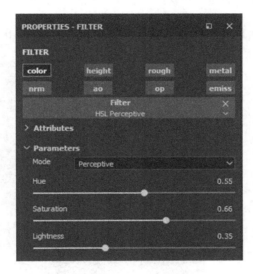

Figure 13-10. *Parameters for modifying HSL Perceptive*

Figure 13-10 shows an example of how you can use the HSL Perceptive filter, but it is not limited to only this type of use. You can easily add this filter to any layer and control the Hue, Saturation, and Lightness values. In Figure 13-11, I have added an empty layer on top of the layer stack with its blending mode set to Passthrough.

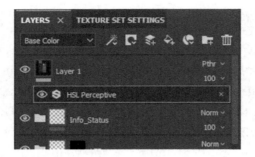

Figure 13-11. *Empty layer with Passthrough blend*

Finally, Figure 13-12 shows the result of the modification done with HSL Perceptive.

Figure 13-12. *Result of HSL Perceptive*

Transform

The Transform filter allows you to move, rotate, and scale the entire contents of a layer. This can be really useful when you want to place some stamped details or add a tile that you created, as shown in Figure 13-13.

Figure 13-13. *Example of the Transform filter*

MatFx Rust Weathering

The MatFx Rust Weathering filter allows you to create procedural rust on a material, as shown in Figure 13-14.

Figure 13-14. *MatFx Rust Weathering filter*

MatFx Edge Wear

The MatFx Edge Wear filter will generate procedural edge damage based on baked maps present in the mesh, as shown in Figure 13-15.

Figure 13-15. *Example of MatFx Edge Wear*

There are more MatFx filters that perform more complex actions that are beyond the scope of this book. You can experiment with them by yourself to understand what they do. Certain effects are old and now not commonly used in workflows. For example, MatFx Water is used rarely, and MatFx Detail Edge Wear has a better alternative called Anchor System. These are a few reasons why I am not covering them here.

Generators

Generators are created in Substance Designer and are used to create procedural effects on masks or materials with respect to the topology of the mesh or baked mesh map. The latest version of Substance Painter ships with 19 generators, and more can be acquired from Substance Share. The 19 base generators are enough when considering all the things you can do with them. But you can easily go to Substance Share to get more if you need something in particular.

Generators are usually applied to the black mask or any mask in particular. A typical setup for a generator in the layer stack looks something like Figure 13-16.

Figure 13-16. *Simple setup for working with generators*

Generators are usually used for creating effects such as dust, wear, damage, etc. Figure 13-17 shows the result created by the setup shown in Figure 13-16.

Figure 13-17. *Dirt generator effect*

Now let's explore some of the commonly used generators in detail and what kind of effects you can create with them.

Dirt Generator

A basic generator generates dust, as the name suggests. Dust most prominently appears on deeper areas of a mesh, especially in the "holes." To use a dirt generator, you will obviously need a base material, which is the surface of the mesh.

In this section, you'll generate dirt on the metallic section of a filter. So, create a Fill layer, which will be the dirt material. Now, in the Fill layer, disable all channels except Color and Roughness. Make the color dark and increase the roughness so that the dirt is less shiny than the metal. The setup should look something like Figure 13-18.

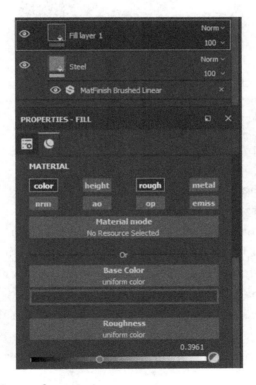

Figure 13-18. *Setup for a generator*

Now right-click the Fill layer and choose "Add black mask." This should make everything specified in the Fill layer disappear from the mesh. Now right-click the mask container and choose "Add generator." Alternatively, you can click the "Add effects" drop-down menu in the Layer Stack window and choose "Add generator" from the list, as shown in Figure 13-19.

Figure 13-19. *Adding a generator*

Now the generator should appear as a sublayer under the mask. Note that the generator will be visible only if you have the mask container selected. If you have selected the layer, then the generator will disappear.

So, the next thing you need to do is add an appropriate generator in the generator container. Make sure the generator sublayer is selected and its properties appear in the Properties window. Right now, there are no generators selected, so you should see a "No generators selected" message displayed on the generator container, as shown in Figure 13-20. Click it and choose "Dirt generator" from the window that appears.

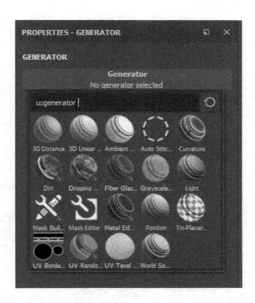

Figure 13-20. *Generator window*

Once you have selected the Dirt generator, its parameters should appear in the Properties window. You can now play around with the parameters to better understand how everything works.

The main parameters that I usually work with are Invert, Dirt Level, Dirt Contrast, Grunge Amount, and Grunge Scale. You can play with these sliders to find the ideal settings that look good to you. See Figure 13-21 for the settings I used.

Invert as the name suggests will simply invert the entire mask. It can be useful in many instances. Dirt level, Grunge amount, and Grunge scale can be used to increase or decrease the amount of dirt, while Dirt contrast will control the blending of the dirt with the material of the surface on which it is applied.

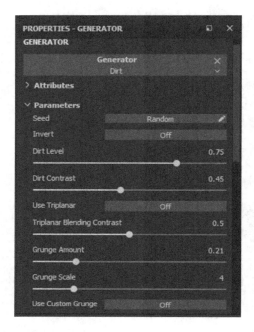

Figure 13-21. *Generator parameters*

Metal Edge Wear Generator

This generator is the go-to solution when edge wear has to be generated on any kind of surface even though the name suggests it is for metals. If you look at any old thing around you, you will notice that the edges are the first to get damaged, or you could say wear out first, whether it is simple discoloration or more prominent damage. This effect can be procedurally generated using the Metal Edge Wear generator, which adds an extra amount of realism to your renders.

Adding it to your surface is as simple as adding a Dirt generator. Add a Fill layer on top of your Material layer and add a black mask to it. Then right-click the mask container and click "Add generator." Now click the empty generator container and choose the Metal Edge Wear generator from the window. Now you can edit the parameters of this generator in the Properties window. See Figure 13-22 and Figure 13-23.

Figure 13-22. *An example of the Metal Edge Wear generator*

Figure 13-23. *Parameters of the Metal Edge Wear generator*

Dripping Rust Generator

The Dripping Rust generator, as the name suggests, creates the effect of dripping rust on a surface. See Figure 13-24 as an example of the effect.

Figure 13-24. *Dripping Rust generator example*

Auto Stitcher

This is an interesting generator that can automatically generate stitches around your meshes. This is fun to experiment with as most stitching work isn't done manually inside Substance Painter. But you can see whether this suits your needs or not. See Figure 13-25.

Figure 13-25. *The Auto Stitch generator*

Mask Builder – Legacy and Mask Editor

Finally, there are the generators Mask Builder – Legacy and Mask Editor. These are complex tools and hard to explain on paper. They are best understood by using them. By now you have seen how generators work, so I highly recommend that you experiment with these two generators so you can understand for yourself how they work.

Mask Builder – Legacy creates a mask that is a combination of edge wear and dirt, as you can see in Figure 13-26. This generator can roughly create the effect of every other generator and has some settings preset for the convenience the user.

Figure 13-26. *An example of Mask Builder – Legacy*

The Mask Editor generator provides a huge amount of control for users, allowing them to create complex procedural masks from scratch using image inputs. This requires more skill and experience to use as there are huge amounts of things that you can do with this. See Figure 13-27.

Figure 13-27. *Result of Mask Editor*

There are more generators that exist, but I mostly use the ones I have covered in this chapter. So, to be proficient with texturing in Substance Painter, you need to have a good command of the generators because they allow users to create complex procedural effects that otherwise are hard to create manually.

Uses of Grunges and Other Procedural Maps

Procedural maps such as grunges and patterns have a ton of applications in Substance Painter. They can be used to create various effects on materials or even create materials from scratch. These are best understood using practical examples, so in this section you will learn how to use the maps in some practical ways to create certain things. But before you do anything, you need to set up your project. First, create a new project, choose CubeTest as a mesh, and use the settings shown in Figure 13-28.

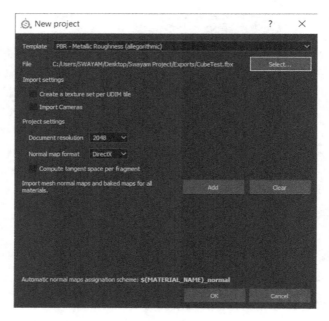

Figure 13-28.   *Project settings*

Now click OK. Next, you need to bake the mesh maps. Open the Texture Set Settings window and then click the Bake Mesh Maps button to launch the Baker window.

In the Baker window, load CubeTest_H as a high poly mesh. Also, set "Output size" to 2048, and set Antialiasing to Subsampling 4x4. Disable the ID channel baker and leave everything else at the defaults. See Figure 13-29.

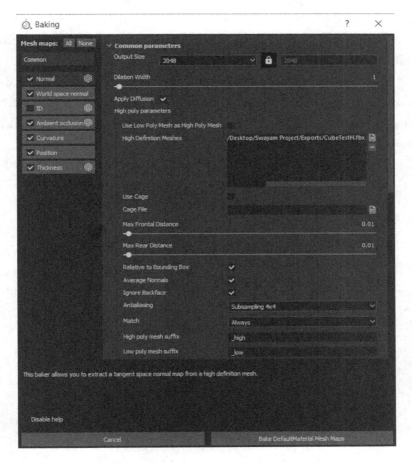

Figure 13-29. Baker settings

Now click Bake and wait for the baking process to finish. Once the baking has finished, go to the layer stack and delete the default Paint layer that is there. Now the project is ready.

Using Patterns as Height

In this section, you'll will learn how to use patterns in conjunction with the Height channel to achieve some interesting results. For this scenario, you will use the scene that you set up before. Go to the layer stack and create a

129

Fill layer. Disable every channel on it except Height. Now in the Shelf, click the Procedurals tab, and you should see a wide range of procedural images available at your disposal. The Height channel in your layer properties should be empty by default, so now you can drag one of these grayscale procedural images and drop them onto the empty channel. In our case, let's use Fabric Diagonal and drag and drop it on the layer channel and increase its scale to 60. See Figure 13-30.

Figure 13-30. *Layer properties for Fill*

Now you should see the result in Figure 13-31.

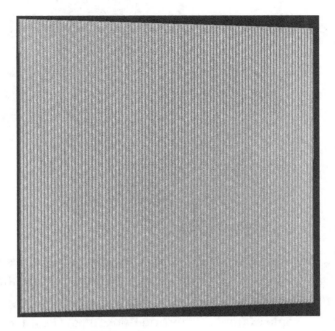

Figure 13-31. *Result of fill so far*

Now let's add some more details to this. Right-click the layer and add a filter. After that, click the empty filter container and choose the Warp filter. Set the Warp intensity to something like 0.4. Now you should have a result somewhat similar to Figure 13-32.

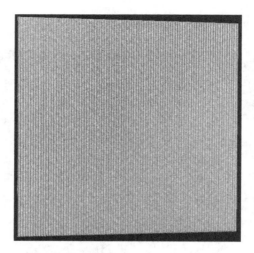

Figure 13-32.   Result after the Warp filter

This now looks like woven fabric. You can add color to it to see how it looks. This was just a small example; you can now try adding other images to the Height input to see what you can come up with.

As another simple example, if you add Bricks 01 to Height, reduce the tiling to 10, and increase the Warp intensity to 0.6, you get the result shown in Figure 13-33.

Figure 13-33.   Procedural example bricks

Patterns as Masks

Another use of patterns is to use them as a mask. Patterns are either grayscale or black-and-white, so they can be easily used as a mask. In this section, you will create an example to see how this works. First create a Fill layer with the Color, Height, Rough, and Metal channels active. Now set the color to golden yellow and the rest of the settings as shown in Figure 13-34. Also rename the layer to **Gold leaves**.

Figure 13-34. *Fill layer parameters*

Now right-click the fill layer and add a black mask. This should make your material disappear. After that, right-click your mask container and click "Add fill." This will add a Fill sublayer to your mask. You will see that this fill layer has only the grayscale input active. This is where you put your grayscale or black-and-white texture. In this case, you can drag and drop any texture of your choice, but for the sake of this example, you'll see how to add the Fabric Fleur De Lis texture to this input slot. Then you should have results similar to Figure 13-35.

Figure 13-35. *Fill result*

Now let's combine what you have learned so far. Select the "Gold leaves" layer and duplicate it; then rename it to **Fabric**. Right-click the mask and click "Invert mask." This should make everything look incorrect, but don't worry about the results right now. Once the mask has been inverted, choose the Fabric layer and change the settings according to Figure 13-36.

Figure 13-36. *Fabric layer settings*

Once that's done, right-click this layer and choose "Add fill." Enable only the Height channel and drag and drop Fabric Diagonal from the Procedurals tab. In the Fill parameters of the Properties window, increase the scale to 55. For texture parameters, refer to Figure 13-37.

Figure 13-37. *Parameters for a procedural texture*

Finally, add the Warp filter with a 0.1 intensity on the Fabric layer. You should now get the result shown in Figure 13-38.

Figure 13-38. *Result so far*

This was just one example; you can now add different procedurals and see what effects you can create. To change the patterns, you need to first click the "Gold leaves" layer and choose its mask. Click the fill layer of the mask where you added the pattern. Drag and drop a different pattern into the grayscale slot. Now click the mask of the Fabric layer and go to the Fill layer of the mask, which holds the pattern. Drag and drop the same pattern that you added in the "Gold leaves" layer, and you should now have a different pattern applied to your mesh.

Figure 13-39 shows an example of another pattern being used.

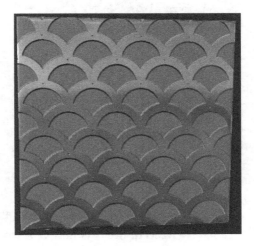

Figure 13-39. *Another example of a procedural pattern*

Procedural Images as Maps

Procedural images can also be used as maps for various purposes. Let's see some examples of this. You have already created a basic base for fabric material. So, now you can add some details to it. Begin by creating a Fill layer with the Color, Height, Rough, and Metal channels active. Set the parameters according to Figure 13-40.

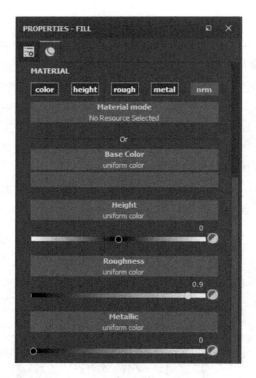

Figure 13-40. *Material parameters for project*

Rename this layer to **Fabric color**. Now create another Fill layer with only the Height channel active and name this **Fabric base**. Add Fabric Diagonal into its Height channel. Increase the scale to 55 and change the texture parameters according to Figure 13-41.

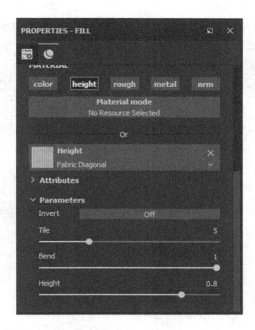

Figure 13-41. *Texture parameters*

Now switch to Height mode in the layer stack by clicking the drop-down menu and choosing Height, as shown in Figure 13-42.

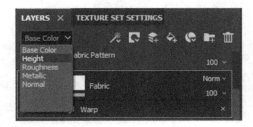

Figure 13-42. *Switching to Height mode in the layer stack*

Once in Height mode, click the blending mode drop-down list for the "Fabric base" layer and choose Subtract. Now you can switch back to Base Color mode in the layer stack. After that, add the Warp filter to the "Fabric base" layer with an intensity of 0.1.

You will now notice that you now have a fabric base, but it lacks variation and details of real fabric. In reality, you will see that fabrics are not a constant color; instead, the color varies. This brings us back to the topic at hand. We are going to use a procedural map to add variation to this base fabric.

So, let's go back to the "Fabric color" layer, right-click it, and choose "Add fill." In the Fill sublayer, enable only the Color channel. Go to the Procedurals tab in the Shelf and search for *Perlin noise*. Now drag and drop the Perlin noise into the color slot of the fill effect that you just created. Increase the scale to 6 and set the texture parameters, as shown in Figure 13-43.

Figure 13-43. *Perlin noise parameters*

Once this is done, click the blending mode of the Fill sublayer, change it to Linear Dodge (Add), and change its blending opacity to a low value, something like 6. Finally, add a Blur filter on top of the fill effect to make the effect of the noise smoother. Right-click the "Fabric color" layer and add a filter. In the empty filter slot, add Blur and change its value to something like 0.2. You may blur by any amount that looks good to you. In the end, you should have a result similar to Figure 13-44.

Figure 13-44. *Final result*

See Figure 13-44, It is an example. Procedural maps can be used as roughness maps as well for creating custom roughness on surfaces. You can test this by dragging and dropping any grunge map from the Procedurals tab directly into the Roughness slot of your layer or into the Roughness slot of a fill effect. There are lots of possibilities; everything depends on experimentation and practice.

I hope that you now have the clear idea about how you can create procedural maps in Substance Painter. In next chapter, you will learn about anchor points and their implementations in Substance Painter.

CHAPTER 14

Substance Anchors

Anchors are another procedural tool of Substance Painter. They allow users to add further details to a mesh without manual labor. In this chapter, you will learn how you can leverage the power of anchors. To be effective at using Substance Painter, it is important to know how they work.

What Is an Anchor?

Anchor points in Substance Painter are user-defined references of certain elements or resources present within the layer stack that can be used later to perform certain actions or operations based on their information. This allows you to effectively link layers or masks and have a single anchor point affect multiple aspects of your project.

Suppose you painted a normal with information in a layer way down somewhere in the layer stack. Now you are adding edge damage and wear to your surface. Substance Painter does not have a direct way of knowing about the existence of that normal information and that some kind of procedural operation has to be performed on it. So, you can add an anchor on the layer that contains the normal information as a reference point that can be called later during the procedural operation to tell Substance Painter that it has to interact with that additional normal map information.

For an anchor system to work, you need to ensure that the anchor point that needs to be referenced is further down in the layer stack than the layer on which it is called. Any anchor point that is above cannot be called by a layer below. See Figure 14-1.

© Abhishek Kumar 2020
A. Kumar, *Beginning PBR Texturing*, https://doi.org/10.1007/978-1-4842-5899-6_14

Figure 14-1. *Adding an anchor point*

An anchor point can be added anywhere in the layer. To add an anchor, simply right-click a layer and navigate to where it says "Add anchor point," and click to add it to your layer. The anchor point will automatically pick the name of the parent layer, but you can certainly change its name at any time by double-clicking it. It's a good habit if you rename layers as you create them, as this will help at a later stage for searching.

Using Anchor Points in a Practical Way

Now let's see some examples of how you can use anchor points in a practical way. But before you do that, you need to set up a project. Once again, you will use a CubeTest for this purpose. This might be a little complex, so follow each step carefully.

We will begin by creating a new project with the settings shown in Figure 14-2. Select CubeTest as the file and set the document resolution to 2048. Also, you can set the normal map format to DirectX even though this does not matter much as you are not going to export this to any external program.

Figure 14-2. *Project settings*

Now click OK, and you are ready to bake some mesh maps. Go to Texture Set Settings and click Bake Mesh Maps to launch the Baker window. Disable the ID setting as you don't have any ID maps, and load CubeTestH as a high poly mesh. See Figure 14-3 for the rest of the settings and then click Bake and wait for the baking process to finish.

Figure 14-3. *Baker settings*

Once baking has finished, you are ready for the next step. Click the default Paint layer that Substance Painter creates and delete it. Now create a Fill layer and rename it to **Base_Mat**. Enable only the Color, Rough, and Metal channels and set its parameters according to Figure 14-4.

Figure 14-4. *Fill layer settings*

These values are not set in stone, and you can change them if you want. Now you need to create a Paint layer with only the Normal channel active. Rename this layer to **Normal_Info**. Make sure that the Normal_Info layer is selected and scroll down in the Properties window to the Alpha settings. Click the X icon in the top-right corner of the Alpha slot to remove it, as shown in Figure 14-5.

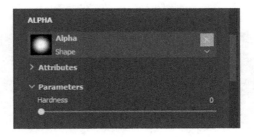

Figure 14-5. *Removing the Alpha slot*

Now scroll down and you should see an empty Normal map slot. You can drag and drop custom normal maps from the Shelf to this slot and use it with a brush to stamp normal map details on your mesh. To see the normal map stamps that ship with Substance Painter, click the Hard Surfaces tab in the Shelf, as shown in Figure 14-6.

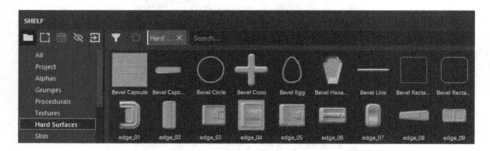

Figure 14-6. *Normal map stamps in the Shelf*

If you want more normal map stamps, you can buy them online. But for our purposes, there are already enough of them. So, drag and drop any map from the Shelf to the Normal map slot in the Properties window. Now your brush should have the stamp attached to it. Click the mesh to see its effect. Once you have made several stamps on the mesh, then proceed to the next step.

Now add another Fill layer with the Color, Height, and Rough channels active and rename it to **Damage**. For the layer settings, refer to Figure 14-7.

Figure 14-7. Fill layer settings

Now add a black mask to the Damage layer and add a generator to it. Choose the Metal Edgewear generator by clicking the Generator slot.

Adjust your generator settings according to Figure 14-8.

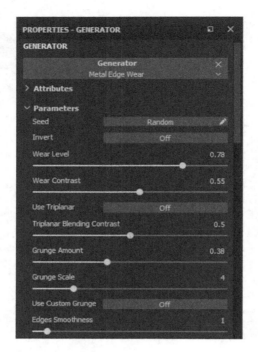

Figure 14-8. *Generator settings*

Now your cube should look somewhat like Figure 14-9.

Figure 14-9. *Result so far*

So far, you can see that the Edge Wear generator is working on the edges of the cube but is not interacting with the normal maps that you have stamped. You want the Edge Wear generator to work on the normal map stamps as well. So for that, you need to use anchor points.

Right-click the Normal_Info layer and then click "Add anchor point." This will add an Anchor Point sublayer on the Normal_Info layer. The anchor point automatically picks the name of the main folder on which it is applied and has an anchor logo to its left. See Figure 14-10.

Figure 14-10. *Anchor point under layer*

Now go back to the Damage layer and click the generator. Scroll down to the generator properties, and you should see an option called Micro Details. See Figure 14-11.

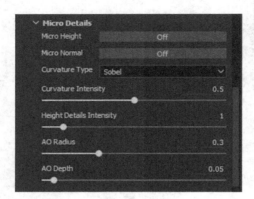

Figure 14-11. *Micro Details settings*

Also, if you scroll further down, you should see two image inputs called Micro Normal and Micro Height. See Figure 14-12.

Figure 14-12. *Micro Normal and Height image inputs*

Click the Micro Normal image input slot, and you should see that a new window opens and has two tabs; one says Resources and another says Anchor Points. Click the Anchor Points tab, which will list all the anchor points that you have created. In this case, it should show only one. See Figure 14-13.

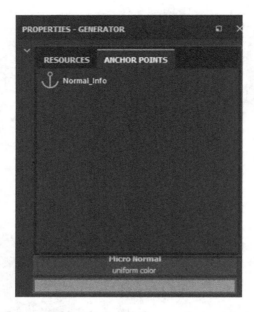

Figure 14-13. *This window lists all the anchor points created*

Click the anchor point that you created in this example; remember, it is named Normal_Info. Now you will see that the normal image input changes into a layer reference. Click the "Referenced channel" drop-down menu, which by default should be referencing Base Color, and change it to Normal. See Figure 14-14.

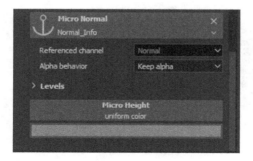

Figure 14-14. *Anchor point referencing anchored layer*

Now scroll up to the Micro Details tab and see where it says Micro Normal; it should say Off by default. Turn it on by clicking it.

As soon as you turn it on, you should see that the Edge Wear generator starts interacting with the normal maps as well. Your final result should look something like Figure 14-15.

Figure 14-15. *Result of using an anchor*

We have barely scratched the surface of what is possible with anchors. You can even paint height maps and use the same method as in this chapter; however, just load an anchor point into the Micro Height input slot and reference the Height channel. When you experiment more with anchor points, you will find that you can create some amazing textures for your meshes.

In the next chapter, I will discuss Iray fundamentals and how to render using the Iray tools.

CHAPTER 15

Rendering with Iray

Iray is a GPU-based render engine developed by Nvidia. It is a physically based, path tracing render engine that uses GPU cores to rapidly render realistic-looking images in high definition. It is built into Substance Painter to help users visualize the final result of the texturing work done on a mesh (see Figure 15-1).

Figure 15-1. *A render created in Iray (image courtesy: Abhishek Kumar)*

A. Kumar, *Beginning PBR Texturing*, https://doi.org/10.1007/978-1-4842-5899-6_15

The Iray renderer can also be used to create portfolio renders as it is a capable render engine that can produce physically correct results. This renderer uses HDRI lighting to generate realistic lighting based on data captured in the real world and calibrated. The background is actually the HDRI environment used to light the scene. You can also change the HDRI environment using the settings.

Launching the Renderer

To launch the renderer, press the keyboard shortcut key F10. Alternatively, you can click the Mode menu and choose Rendering (Iray) from the list. Or you can click the camera icon in the Viewport menu in the top-right corner of the window.

Renderer Settings

There are various render settings that you can modify to personalize your renders. The Iray renderer also supports various types of post-processing effects that can be used to greatly enhance any render. The background HDRI environment can be modified and changed as well if needed.

When you launch the Iray renderer, you will see the Renderer Settings window, as shown in Figure 15-2. (Pressing F9 will switch back to normal viewport or Painting mode.)

Various global and shader settings will affect the render result, but first, let's begin with the most basic settings provided after switching to Render mode by pressing the F10 key.

Figure 15-2. *Renderer Settings window*

This window allows you to modify for how long you want to render and in how many samples you want to render. *Samples* here means iterations. The more samples, the better the result. Basically, you can specify the maximum samples that you want in your render and for how long you want the renderer to run. When one of these settings is achieved, meaning either the renderer reaches the maximum sample count or the maximum time, then the renderer will stop.

The caustic sampler can be enabled if you want your render to have a caustic effect. The Firefly filter is always turned on as its task is to remove white spots that appear during the render, which is an unwanted artifact. The resolution settings allow you to change the resolution of the rendered image that you save to your disk. The Share button allows you to directly upload your current render to ArtStation, which is an online portfolio web site.

Here are the other settings available:

- **Display Settings**: Display Settings allow you to modify the Environment, Camera, and Viewport settings that alter how your renders look but do not modify your textures in any way Figure 15-3.

Figure 15-3. *Display Settings*

- **Environment Settings**: This allows you to modify or change the background HDRI map. You can modify its Exposure, which increases/decreases the brightness of lights in the scene. Or you can rotate it to change the light direction. You can also change the HDRI map to completely alter the lighting of the scene. You can do this by clicking the Environment Map option. There are a multitude of other options available that you can play with to see what suits your render best.

- **Camera Settings**: As obvious by the name, this setting allows users to modify the various features of the camera being used to render the scene. Users can change the camera's Field of view, Focal length, Focus distance, and Aperture, as shown in Figure 15-4. Also, the Post-Process effects can be activated from here to further enhance the renders.

Figure 15-4. *Camera Settings*

- **Viewport Settings**: This has all the settings related to displaying your mesh in the viewport, as shown in Figure 15-5. You can increase/decrease Anisotropic Filtering or MipMap bias and not much else when it comes to rendering. This is mostly dedicated to displaying mesh in Painting mode.

Figure 15-5. *Viewport Settings*

- **Shader Settings**: This will let you change or modify the shader that you are using. Shaders are just mathematical functions, and they have lots of exposed parameters that you can modify to alter how your textures look by changing the way light interacts with them. You can also change which Shader you are using by clicking the large button that displays your current shader name. By default the "pbr-metal-rough" shader, as shown in Figure 15-6, is selected.

Figure 15-6. *Shader settings*

In the next chapter, I will discuss the procedure to export the created material from Substance Painter to other applications such as Marmoset, Maya, and Blender.

CHAPTER 16

Integrating with Blender, Maya and Marmoset

Exporting files from Maya and Blender for use in Substance Painter is pretty straightforward. Substance can import most major file types including .fbx and .obj, which can be created by all 3D modeling applications. For our purposes, we will use the .fbx type for exporting files for use in Substance Painter.

To export files for use in Substance Painter, you will usually have one high poly model from which you will bake maps into a low poly model. If you are not creating your own mesh for games, then you can directly texture the high poly model.

One important thing that you need to keep in mind while exporting anything for use in Substance Painter is that your mesh needs to be properly UV mapped with no faces overlapping or leaving the 0-1 space. Also, each UV island should have enough texel density to correctly display the textures. UDIM tiles can also be used in supported programs, and Substance will create a new texture set for every UDIM tile it finds.

© Abhishek Kumar 2020
A. Kumar, *Beginning PBR Texturing*, https://doi.org/10.1007/978-1-4842-5899-6_16

Low Poly and High Poly Workflow

If you want to export both low poly and high poly models, then you need to keep certain things in mind. First you need to ensure that both low poly and high poly models are in the world origin and are overlapping each other. This means they should be at the same point as Substance Painter casts rays with reference to their position and should bake information from high poly to low poly mesh based on their position. If they are not in the same spot, then there will be errors in the bake (Figure 16-1).

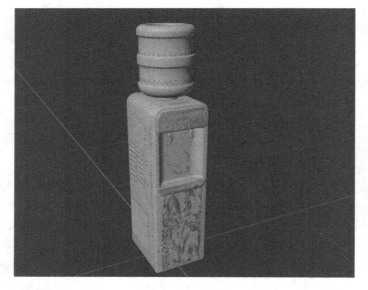

Figure 16-1. *Both high poly and low poly are in same place*

In Figure 16-1 you can see that both low poly models and high poly models are in the same place such that they overlap each other and start z-fighting. This may look odd, but since they are in separate layers, they can be exported individually while staying in the same place. And yes, the low poly model and high poly model both are exported separately.

Naming meshes for baking is important (unless you decide to exolode the mesh, which we will discuss later). As you have seen before, baking in Substance Painter happens through an option called Match; this option has two types. One is called Always, and another one is called By Mesh Name. Baking parts of the mesh that are close together can cause shading issues. So, you can either name mesh parts appropriately or explode the mesh.

Naming mesh parts should be done in a comprehensible way, and each part of the high poly model should have same name as its corresponding low poly part. The _low and _high suffixes should appear in the names. See Figure 16-2 as an example of how naming is done.

Figure 16-2. *Naming conventions for baking*

Now, if you have named your mesh properly, then Match: By Mesh Name should work correctly and save you from any shading artifacts caused by parts of the mesh that are too close.

Exploding a mesh works in a similar way. *Exploding* a mesh (Figure 16-3) means separating each part that is not connected by faces and laying them so that, during baking, close together parts don't introduce baking artifacts.

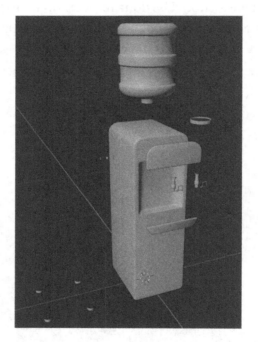

Figure 16-3. *An exploded mesh*

If you have exploded your mesh, then you can bake with the Match: Always setting and your bake should be error-free.

There are a lot of other things to keep in mind as well such as your low poly model should match the high poly model as closely as possible. Your low poly and high poly models should be roughly the same size.

Blender to Substance Workflow

Make sure you have done all the previous preparations, as mentioned previously. Make sure only the layer that contains a low poly model is enabled and select everything visible (Figure 16-4) by clicking and dragging a box around everything.

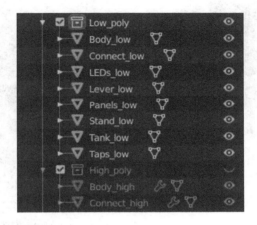

Figure 16-4. *Visibility off and on*

After completing these steps, select File ➤ Export ➤ FBX. Once you click FBX, the export window will open (Figure 16-5).

Figure 16-5. *Default exporter window of Blender*

In the bottom-left menu, you will find a lot of settings that you can modify before exporting your file out of Blender. Select the Selected Objects checkbox and click Mesh so that only Mesh is highlighted, instead of everything. This part of the menu should look like Figure 16-6.

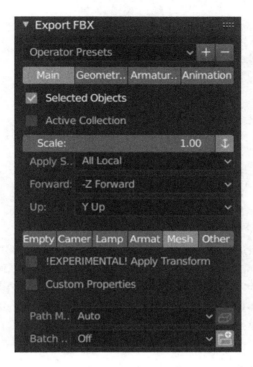

Figure 16-6. *Export settings*

Now click the Geometries tab in the window. There should be a Smoothing option, and by default it should be set to Normals Only. See Figure 16-7.

Figure 16-7. *Geometries tab and Smoothing option*

To export a file for use in Substance Painter, the default Smoothing option Normals Only should work fine, but sometimes you may need to set it to Face. Experimentation is the best strategy here.

Now set your name for the file; let's say in this case you name it **Filter_low**. Select the export destination and click Export.

Now do the same for the high poly model. Hide the low poly model by clicking the eye icon on the folder containing it. Unhide the high poly model by clicking the closed eye icon, and it should be visible again. Now select everything and export them as well.

For simple models, this export method works well, but if your model is complex and has multiple UVs, then you should assign different materials to each of its parts (Figure 16-8).

Figure 16-8. *Blender material editor*

You can create a new material by clicking the + icon and then clicking the New button. Select the material you want to apply on your mesh by selecting it from the list and clicking Assign after selecting the surface on which you want to assign it.

Now you can export, and once you import the file into Substance, a new texture set will be created for each new material.

Maya to Substance Painter Workflow

All the concepts that we discussed for Blender apply to Maya as well. The only thing that is slightly different is the method of exporting. Select everything that you want to export, in this case, the low poly model of the filter. Then select File ➤ Export Selection.

Note   Before exporting your object from Maya, make sure you delete the type history and then freeze and reset the transformation.

Click the "File type" drop-down menu (Figure 16-9) and choose "FBX export" from the list. Now click the Export Selection button (Figure 16-10), and a new window will open.

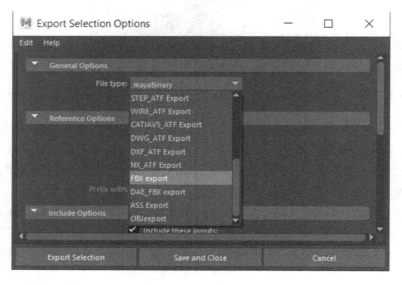

Figure 16-9. *Maya export window*

In this new window, name your file appropriately so that it is easy to identify. Then choose the output directory where you want your file to be exported. Click Export to export your scene as an .fbx file in the desired location.

Figure 16-10. *Export selection window*

This method of exporting files for use in Substance Painter remains universal for almost all software. The only thing that changes is the interface and slightly varied names of tools. So, if you want to send your scene/model to Substance Painter, then I highly recommend that you simply export it as an .obj or .fbx file, and it should be easily transferrable to Substance Painter.

Once again, I would like to stress that files that need to go to Substance Painter need to UV mapped properly and named properly if needed. To avoid shading errors, you can separate each part of the mesh as an object and name the objects appropriately with the correct suffix. Alternatively, meshes can be "exploded" so that during baking no errors occur.

If everything is done accordingly, then you will have no problem importing a file into Substance Painter and also getting a clean bake, which is very important.

Importing into Blender, Maya, and Marmoset

So, you have now exported files for use in Substance Painter and have done some texturing. Now you want to export the file to your preferred render engine to create some renders or maybe integrate it into a scene. Whatever your end goal may be, your first target is to export your textures for whichever render engine you want to use.

Exporting from Substance for Use in Blender

To go from Substance to Blender, you will begin by exporting some textures for use in Blender. Once a model has been textured, Substance can bake all the textures into UVs of the models, and then only the texture maps need to be exported. These texture maps can be exported into the 3D modeling and rendering application of your choice. But remember, different programs require different maps for rendering. We will see this in detail now.

Once you have finished your texturing work and want to export your creation, then select File ➤ Export Textures or press the shortcut key combination Ctrl+Shift+E. This will launch the export window of Substance Painter (Figure 16-11).

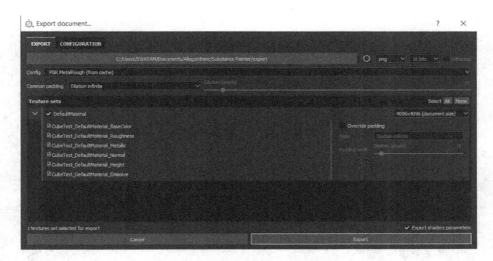

Figure 16-11. *Export window of Substance Painter*

Before you click Export, you'll see there is a multitude of options that allow you to personalize your export for the render/game engine you want to import it into. Click the Configuration tab to see all the options available (Figure 16-12).

Figure 16-12. *Export configuration*

Now for the convenience of the user, the exporter of Substance Painter has some template configurations with preset settings that make the exporting process easier and faster (Figure 16-13). But as of now, there is no template for Blender.

Figure 16-13. *Configuration templates available in Substance Painter*

The best configuration for Blender is PBR MetalRough because Blender is a physically based render engine and uses metallic and roughness maps for rendering. One thing to note here, though, is that Blender uses OpenGL normal maps. This means while creating a project, you need to set the normal map format to OpenGL. You can also use the "Converted maps" section of the export configuration to create maps that you did not work with here but that work with the metallic-roughness workflow.

Now let's export our maps for use in Blender. First click the Config drop-down menu and choose PBR MetalRough from the list. Then choose your output destination. Now click the image format drop-down list (see Figure 16-14) and choose the "bmp" format (or any other image format you want). By default, it should be set to png.

Figure 16-14. *Image format menu*

After that, set the document size to be 2048x2048. Now click the configuration tab and choose PBR MetalRough from the presets list. Right-click PBR MetalRough in the presets list and click Duplicate. This should create a PBR MetalRough_copy preset at the end of the list. Right-click it and rename it to **Blender**.

In the "Output maps" list, delete BaseColor by clicking the small X button at the bottom of the map name. Now create a new RGB file by clicking the RGB button at the top where it says Create (Figure 16-15).

Figure 16-15. *Creating a new output channel*

You will notice that output maps in Substance Painter have a pretty complex naming convention. You need to name your newly created map similarly. Either you can read the name of one of the maps shown and type it in or you can copy the entire name of one of the maps shown, let's say $mesh_$textureSet_Normal, and paste it into the name slot of your newly created map and then replace *Normal* at the end with *Diffuse*.

Now go to the "Converted maps" list and drag and drop Normal OpenGL into the RGB map slot of the Normal output map. A new menu should open as soon as you release your mouse (see Figure 16-16). But remember that if you have not created your project with an OpenGL normal configuration, then the export will fail.

Figure 16-16. *Changing the Normal map output type*

Choose RGB Channels from the list. This should change the Normal map output type to OpenGL. Now you need to drag and drop Diffuse from the "Converted maps" list to the new Diffuse output map slot that you created. This time, again choose RGB Channels from the list that appears.

You can remove the Emissive and Height channels as you don't need them unless you have created something specific that uses those channels. You final output channel list should look something like Figure 16-17.

Figure 16-17. *Output maps list*

Now you can go back to the Export tab, choose your destination, and click Export.

This should create all the required maps for you in the directory that you chose. Those maps can now be imported into Blender and set up to work with their respective meshes, something that you will learn how to do in upcoming chapter.

Exporting from Substance for Use in Maya

Exporting files for use in Maya is not very different; in fact, it is much simpler. In this section, you will export for one of the latest render engines introduced to work with Maya: Arnold. Substance Painter has a preset for that render engine, so this will make exporting fast. The preset that you are going to use is "Arnold 5 (AiStandard)," as shown in Figure 16-18.

In the export window, click the Config presets drop-down menu and choose Arnold 5 (AiStandard) from the list.

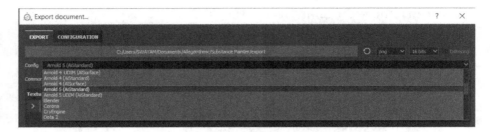

Figure 16-18. *Arnold 5 preset in Config presets list*

If you go to the configuration settings and take a look at the Arnold 5 (AiStandard) preset, you will see that it is similar to the PBR MetalRough preset (see Figure 16-19). This is because the Arnold 5 render engine is also a PBR-based render engine that uses the metallic-roughness workflow. That is why the maps queued for export are the same as the PBR MetalRough preset (except the normal map that will be exported in the OpenGL format).

In this particular case, you could have exported the textures in the PBR MetalRough preset as well. This would have been fine except that you would need to change the normal map format.

Figure 16-19. *Configuration preset for Arnold 5 (AiStandard)*

Now switch back to the Export tab because we need to change some more settings here as well. First change the bit depth of the "png" setting to 16 bit and change the document resolution to 2048x2048 (Figure 16-20).

Figure 16-20. *Export settings*

Make sure you choose the correct directory where you want your exported maps to be saved. Also, make it a practice to name files properly so that they are easy to identify and work with.

That's all for the Maya export process; you are now ready to import the materials into Maya and set up the textures. In the next chapter, I'll discuss the process of importing maps into the render engine of your choice and rendering a portfolio-ready image.

Note   Remember that the naming convention is important for each object and material.

Exporting from Substance for Use in Marmoset Toolbag

Exporting textures for use in Marmoset Toolbag is no different from the others that I covered previously except that some of the settings will change. So, let's see what we need to do.

The first thing that you need to do before you begin texturing is to know what your target render engine is. If it is Marmoset Toolbag 3, then it supports both the specular-glossiness and metallic-roughness workflows. This is a huge advantage as you can create your textures in any format and easily bring them over to Marmoset to create renders. But in this section, you will learn to export using the specular-glossiness workflow to get a taste of it. However, you can also export using the metallic-roughness workflow if you want.

Once again, you will launch the exporter window and click the Config presets drop-down menu. Choose PBR SpecGloss from MetalRough from the list (Figure 16-21).

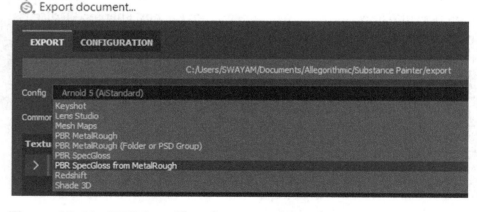

Figure 16-21. *PBR SpecGloss from MetalRough option*

This will convert your metallic-roughness maps to specular-glossiness maps during export so that you can export them into Marmoset Toolbag. Marmoset Toolbag uses the DirectX normal map format, so there are no problems there.

You can switch to the Configuration tab to see which maps are selected for export (see Figure 16-22).

Figure 16-22. *Configuration for PBR SpecGloss from MetalRough option*

These maps are used by Marmoset Toolbag for creating PBR renders, so we will export them. Once again switch back to the Export tab and set your export destination. Then change the rest of the settings according to Figure 16-23.

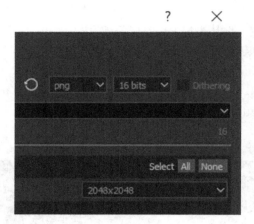

Figure 16-23. *Image parameters for export*

Once you're done, you can click Export.

In the next chapter, I will discuss the process of importing maps in the render engine of your choice and show how to render a portfolio-ready image.

CHAPTER 17

Rendering a Portfolio

Rendering is the last stage in the 3D computer graphics production pipeline. In computer graphics, rendering is the computation process involved to convert three-dimensional objects into 2D images or a series of images.

We can divide rendering into two categories.

- Offline rendering

- Real-time rendering

Generally, we use offline rendering, to convert a 3D scene into a super-realistic image. It can take a huge amount of time to render the image while using real-time, or online, rendering computation very fast and interactively. Commonly we use offline rendering for movies and commercials and online rendering for the game industry.

Integration with Blender

In this section, I'll cover how you can use your created maps with Blender. I will use the Cycles render engine at the beginning, and after that, I will show how you can use your maps with the EEVEE render engine (Figure 17-1). Let's see first how to change the render engine inside Blender. As this book is specifically based on high-end texturing, you should already be familiar with the interface and tools of Blender; therefore, I am not going to explore them in detail here.

© Abhishek Kumar 2020
A. Kumar, *Beginning PBR Texturing*, https://doi.org/10.1007/978-1-4842-5899-6_17

Figure 17-1. *Blender GUI (source:* `https://www.blender.org/`*)*

Click the camera icon in the Properties window of Blender. The first option should be Render Engine with a drop-down list that allows you to change your current render engine. Click that drop-down menu and choose Cycles (Figure 17-2).

Figure 17-2. *Switching the render engine in Blender*

Now that you have chosen your render engine, let's see how materials work in Blender. To use materials first, you will need a UV unwrapped mesh (Figure 17-3). If your mesh is not UV mapped, then you can get away with some procedural materials, but any material containing patterns or any kind of visual information will be warped.

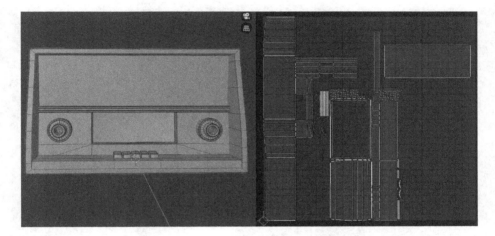

Figure 17-3. *UV unwrapped model that we will use in this chapter*

Once you have a UV mapped model loaded into your viewport, then your Properties window should show a multitude of new options. Clicking the checkered circle toward the bottom of the Properties window opens a material's properties tab, where you will see all the available material parameters. At first, this tab should be empty with only the New button at the top of the window. Click it to create a new material.

You should see a Use Nodes option highlighted in the window (Figure 17-4). This is important for you here because we will focus on creating materials in the node editor.

Figure 17-4. *Material parameters*

You can also set up your materials in this Properties window by clicking the small white circle next to each texture input slot. When you click the circle icon, a new window should open, giving you a list of operations that can be performed. From that list, choose the Image Texture option and then load the correct images into their respective slots (Figure 17-5).

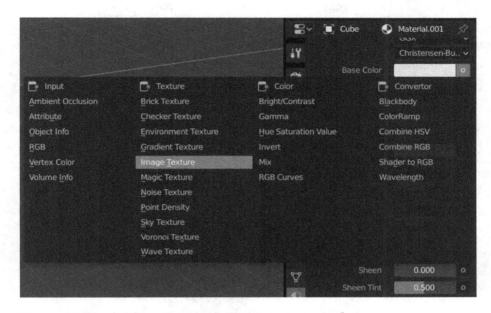

Figure 17-5. *Adding image texture to a texture slot*

Once you have selected the Image Texture option, you will see new inputs and parameters (Figure 17-6).

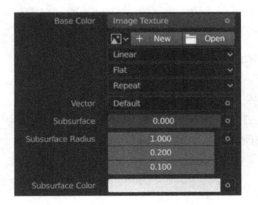

Figure 17-6. *Image texture parameters*

Now click the Open option to launch the file browser and navigate to the correct image that you want to load in that texture slot. Once you have loaded all the textures in their respective slots, then your model will be ready for rendering. But I don't prefer this method because this does not give us the flexibility to edit the textures. So, we will do our material setup in the node editor. To open the node editor, place your pointer on the junction between the Properties window and the viewport until your pointer turns into a two-headed arrow. Then right-click and choose Vertical Split (Figure 17-7).

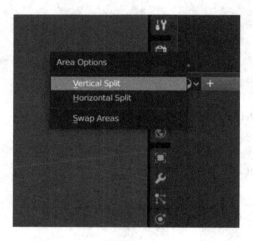

Figure 17-7. *Splitting the workspace*

Your workspace will now split, so you now have two 3D workspaces. Click the Editor Type drop-down menu icon at the top-left corner of your window and choose Shader Editor from the list (Figure 17-8).

Figure 17-8. *Changing the viewport type*

Now your new editor section should change into a shader editor (Figure 17-9). You can edit how your textures work with the help of mathematical nodes. By default, a Principled BSDF shader is applied to your model when you use a material. You can, of course, change this at any time either from the material properties editor by changing the surface type or from the shader editor by deleting the default Principled BSDF shader and adding another shader node.

193

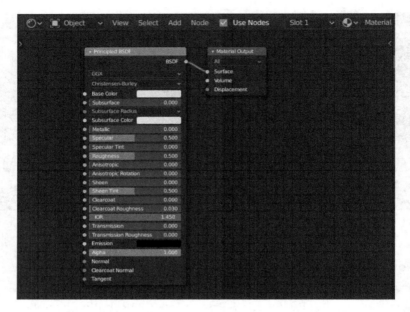

Figure 17-9. *Shader editor in Blender*

To add a new shader, you can press Shift+A, and this will open a new menu that allows you to choose which node you want to add to your tree. There are several categories from which you can choose nodes. In our case, we will mostly use the Shader category to add new shaders, the Textures category to add image textures, and sometimes the Vectors category (Figure 17-10).

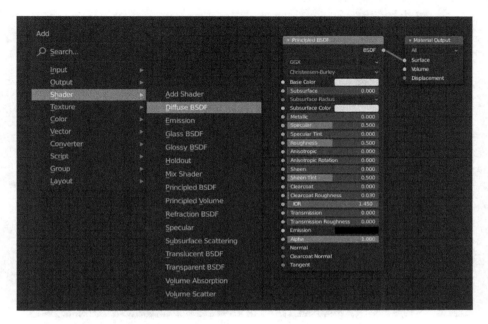

Figure 17-10. *Adding new shaders/nodes*

If you are unable to find a node or don't know which category it falls into, then you can use the search function located at the top of the menu. You can type in the name of the node that you want to add, and it will find it for you.

So, you are now ready to set up your material inside Blender. First, you need to import all the required textures. Press Shift+A to open the Add menu and then select Texture ➤ Image Texture. This will add the Image Texture node to your node tree, and in the Image Texture node there should be an option called Open. Click it to open the file browser (Figure 17-11).

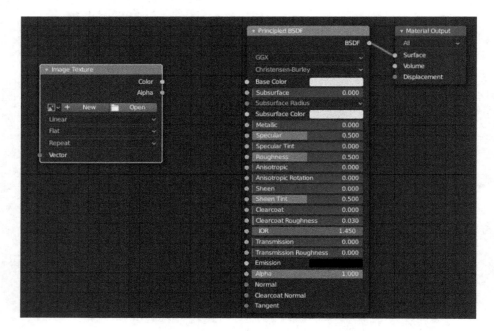

Figure 17-11. *Image Texture node in the tree*

In the file browser, navigate to where you have exported your textures. The first one that we are going to import is the Diffuse map. Select it and choose Open Image, and it will load into Blender. Now click and drag a connection from the output of the Image Texture node and connect it to the BaseColor input of the Principled BSDF node (Figure 17-12).

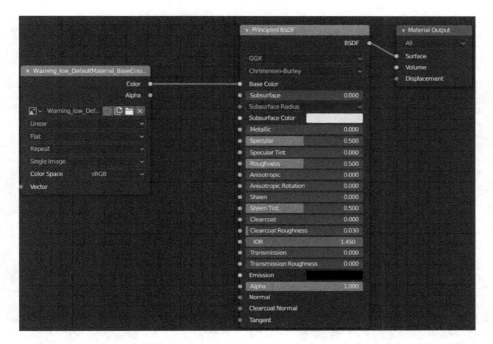

Figure 17-12. *Connecting nodes*

When the nodes are connected, the output from one node should be connected to the input of another node via a white connection. You need to connect other texture inputs in similar way.

Now duplicate the Image Texture node by selecting it and pressing Shift+D, or create a new one. If you duplicate the node, then your image input will already be populated by the Diffuse texture that you imported earlier. Click the X icon to remove it. Now you should have a clean node. Next import the Roughness map for the texture. Once it's imported, you may connect it to the Roughness input of the Principled BSDF shader. We also need to change the color space of the Roughness map. To do that, click the drop-down menu in front of Color Space; by default, it should be set to sRGB. Change it to Non-Color.

Now we need to import the metalness map. For that, follow the same steps again. Either create a new node or copy the previous one and delete the unwanted image. Once the image has been imported, we will change

197

its color space to Non-Color as well. Then connect the output to the input of Metallic of Principled BSDF.

Lastly, we will import the normal map and change its color space to Non-Color as well. Also, we need to create a Normal Map node. The output of the Image Texture node containing the normal map will connect to the input of the normal map node, and then the output of the normal map node will connect with the Normal input of Principled BSDF node. The setup so far should look something like Figure 17-13.

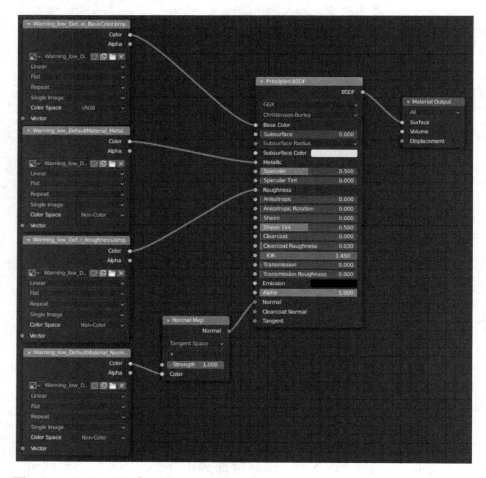

Figure 17-13. *Node setup*

This should be good enough for creating a render of your mesh in Blender. Even though this is a quick and dirty setup, this still gets the job done pretty well. If you want, you can create more complex node setups that allow you to modify the textures beyond what is already created.

For a quick render setup, create a Sun lamp by pressing Shift+A in the 3D viewport and selecting Light ➤ Sun (Figure 17-14).

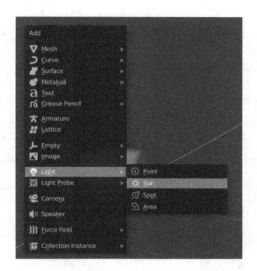

Figure 17-14. *Adding a Sun lamp to a scene*

Then raise it up and rotate it to an angle and also increase the intensity of Sun to 7 from the properties editor. Make the color of the sun slightly yellowish.

Now create a large ground plane and apply a white, slightly shiny material to it. If done correctly, your scene will be ready for rendering. You can also render without a camera by pressing the Z key and switch to the rendered view. This will initiate viewport rendering, but this does not produce good-quality renders. The best way to render is by using a camera.

Create a camera and then move and rotate it to align it the way you want. Then either press F12 on keyboard, which is the shortcut key for rendering, or click the Render button and click Render Image (Figure 17-15).

Figure 17-15. *Render Image option*

For the best render results, you can increase the render samples of the camera from the Scene properties in the properties editor (Figure 17-16). You will probably need several thousand samples and pretty powerful PC for rendering decently complex scenes in a reasonable time.

Figure 17-16. *Scene properties*

But before you render, you can change a few settings to help increase the render speed. First go to Edit ➤ Preferences ➤ System and at the top of the window there should be the option Cycles Render Devices. By default it should be set to None, but if you have a Nvidia GPU, set it to CUDA, or if you have AMD GPU, then set it to OpenCL (Figure 17-17).

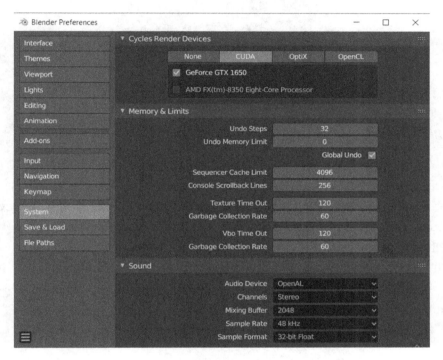

Figure 17-17. *Changing the Cycles render device*

Then save your preferences.

If you look at the Scene properties now, you should see the Devices option is now active. By default it should be set to CPU. Click it and change it to GPU Compute (Figure 17-18).

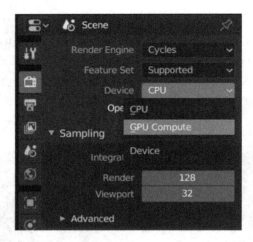

Figure 17-18. *Changing the render device*

The computation of the GPU is always faster if you have a high-performing graphics card. Also, if you look at the Sampling section, these options are currently set to the default values that are more or less preview values. The viewport samples will increase the render iterations when switching to Rendering mode in the viewport, while the render samples will increase render iterations when rendering with a camera.

A higher value for Sampling will result in better render results but a longer compute duration (Figure 17-19).

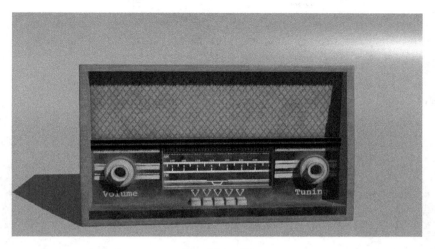

Figure 17-19. *Render created in Blender*

Integration with Maya

Now let's see how to use Substance Painter maps with Maya. For this project, we will use the Arnold 5 renderer. Arnold 5 is a physically based ray tracing render engine that ships with Maya and is used for creating high-quality renders for movies (Figure 17-20).

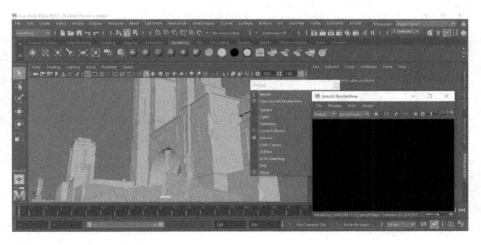

Figure 17-20. *3D model into Maya*

So, as you can tell, it is a powerful render engine that is used in a production environment. You will learn how you can use it to create renders for you.

Let's bring in a mesh by dragging it from a folder and dropping it into the viewport of Maya (Figure 17-21).

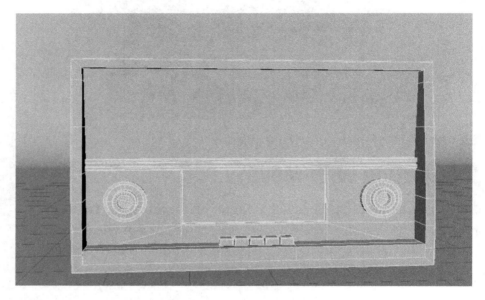

Figure 17-21. *Imported model in Maya*

First, you need to apply an Arnold material to the mesh. To do that, select your mesh and right-click. In the menu that appears, scroll down and select Assign New Material (Figure 17-22).

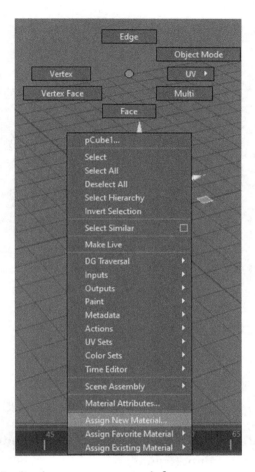

Figure 17-22. *Assigning a new material*

A new window should open asking you which material you want to apply to your mesh. Click Shader under the Arnold heading, and from the shader list on the right, choose aiStandardSurface (Figure 17-23).

Figure 17-23. *Applying the aiStandardSurface shader*

After you have applied the shader, then some new parameters should appear in the attribute editor (Figure 17-24).

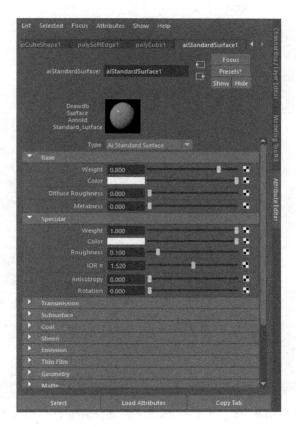

Figure 17-24. *Attribute editor*

We need to plug in our maps in the texture slots present in the attribute editor. So, let's begin with the base color. Click the small checkered square in the Color input. This should launch a new window called Create Render Node. Choose File from the list of options available (Figure 17-25).

Figure 17-25.   *Create Render Node window*

Once you choose File, you will notice that the attribute editor changes. You'll see some file attributes that you will work with (Figure 17-26).

Figure 17-26.   *File attributes*

Click the folder icon toward the right of Image Name. This will launch the file browser. Navigate to your BaseColor map and click Open. This will load in the texture map into Maya. To go back to the attribute editor with texture inputs, click the button highlighted by the red circle in Figure 17-27.

Figure 17-27. *Going back to the attribute editor*

You may not be able to see the effect of the BaseColor map that you applied to the mesh. This is because by default the texture display is turned off. You can enable the texture display by pressing 6 on your alphanumeric keypad.

Now let's import the other maps. On the Base tab there is a Metalness input. Click the small white check box next to the Metalness input. This will again open the Create Render Node window, where you should choose File. Once again, your attribute editor will change. Click the small folder icon next to Image Name, and this will launch the file browser. Choose the metallic map and click Open. This will load the metallic map into Maya. Once you're done, click the drop-down menu next to Color Space. By default it should be set to sRGB, so choose RAW from the list (Figure 17-28).

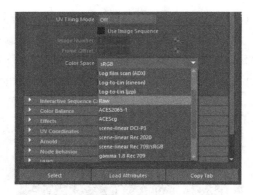

Figure 17-28. *Changing the color space of the map*

Once that's done, go back to the attribute editor with the image inputs. You will import the Roughness map next. The Roughness map needs to be imported into the Roughness input under the Specular heading (Figure 17-29).

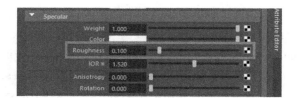

Figure 17-29. *Roughness input*

Once again, click the small checkered box and do exactly what you have been doing for the past couple of textures. Choose File in the Create Render Node window. Then in the new editor, click the small folder icon, and in the file browser window navigate to your Roughness map and click Open to import the image into Maya. Now change Color Space to RAW for this as well, and you are done.

Now let's import the normal map. This will be slightly different from others that you have imported so far. First, you will find the normal map under the Geometry item; it is named Bump Mapping (Figure 17-30).

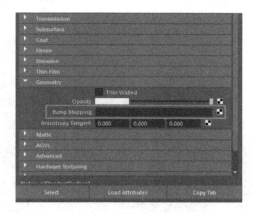

Figure 17-30. *Bump Mapping input*

Click the small checkered box and choose File. This will change the attribute editor into the Bump2D window. Click the drop-down menu next to where it says Use As. By default, it is set to Bump, but for our case we will change it to Tangent Space Normals (Figure 17-31).

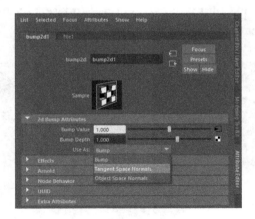

Figure 17-31. *Changing the use type*

Now click the black box with the arrow next to Bump Value; this will take you to the file selection. Again, click the familiar folder icon, and that will open the file browser. Navigate to the normal map that you want to

211

import. Then after selecting it, click Open. This will load your normal map; once again, change its color space to RAW. Now your normal map has been set up as well. Go back to the editor with texture inputs.

Before you render, you need to change one more thing. Click the box with the arrow icon next to the Metalness input (see Figure 17-32).

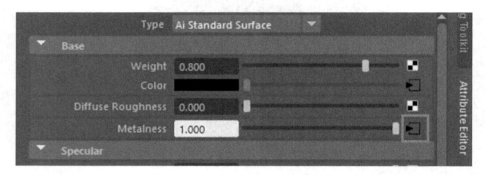

Figure 17-32. *Metalness icon*

Now expand the Color Balance heading and look for Alpha Is Luminance. Select this box to activate it (Figure 17-33).

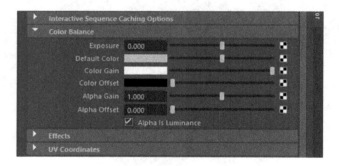

Figure 17-33. *Alpha Is Luminance box*

Do the same for the Roughness map. After that, your file is ready for rendering. A simple setup can be similar to what you used in Blender. There is a large ground plane and some Arnold lights.

To do this, click the Arnold tab on the Shelf of Maya (Figure 17-34).

Figure 17-34. *Shelf of Maya*

You can either create a couple of Area lights (first icon on the left) and try adjusting their parameters to achieve the desired lighting or create a SkyDome light (fourth icon from the left) to create an HDRI-based lighting environment. If you have good-quality HDRI images, then you can create light quickly. For our case, we will create a SkyDome light; you can get some free high-quality HDRI images from Hdrihaven.com. Once you have downloaded an HDRI image that you like, you can click the small checkered square next to Color in the SkyDomeLight attributes window and choose Image from the list. In the new window that appears, click the small folder icon next to File Name, and file browser window will open. From there, navigate to your HDRI image file and load it into Maya. This will apply the texture to the SkyDome light. Your SkyDome light should now appear textured with the HDRI image that you applied to it (Figure 17-35).

Figure 17-35. *The scene with the HDRI SkyDome light*

Your scene is ready for rendering now. Click the Arnold tab in the menu bar and click Render (Figure 17-36).

Figure 17-36. *Rendering the scene*

Note that your scene will render from the view camera that you are using to view your scene. So, set your angle first so that you are properly viewing your model (Figure 17-37).

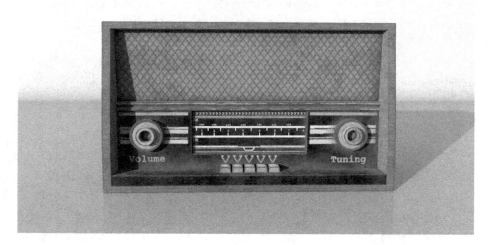

Figure 17-37. *Final render in Maya*

Integration with Marmoset Toolbag

You already exported your textures for Marmoset Toolbag in a previous chapter, so now all that remains is to import those textures into Marmoset. First, we will be using the latest version of the software, which currently is Marmoset Toolbag 3 (Figure 17-38).

Figure 17-38. *Marmoset Toolbag GUI (source:* `https://marmoset.` `co/toolbag/`*)*

Marmoset is a dedicated real-time rendering, animation, and baking program, but it is primarily used by artists to create portfolio-ready renders by using its powerful real-time render engine. We are going to do the same, so let's launch Marmoset Toolbag 3 and start working.

You will import your test mesh by dragging and dropping it onto the interface of Marmoset Toolbag (Figure 17-39).

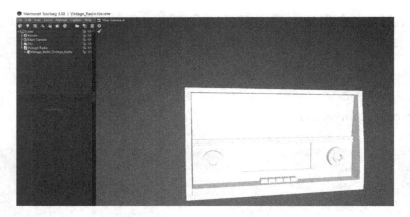

Figure 17-39. *File when imported into Marmoset Toolbag*

Now create a new material by clicking the button shown in Figure 17-40.

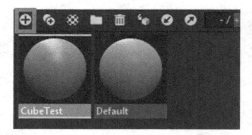

Figure 17-40. *Creating a new material*

Name it **CubeTest**.

Doing that will place the mesh in the center of the screen. Now, before you bring in the textures, you will change a few things. Now change Microsurface from Roughness to Glossiness (Figure 17-41).

Figure 17-41. *Changing the input type*

Change Reflectivity from Metalness to Specular. Now you are ready to import. To import, click the checkered icon to launch the file browser (Figure 17-42).

Figure 17-42. *Checkered map button for importing a texture map*

You need to import the correct texture maps into the correct slots like this. Then drag and drop the material from the tray to the cube. Immediately you will see the effect of your texture. There is no waiting for rendering as everything is in real time. You can change some settings to get the render that you want. You can change the sky settings by clicking Sky in the outliner (Figure 17-43).

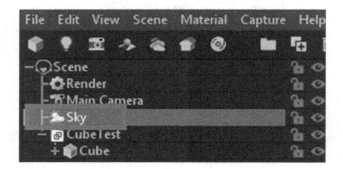

Figure 17-43. *Selecting Sky from the outliner*

Now click Presets to choose from a list of available skies for the lighting environment. After you are satisfied, you can press F11 to save a render (Figure 17-44).

Figure 17-44. *Final render from Marmoset Toolbag*

You should now have a clear understanding of how to use the setup render in Blender, Maya, and Marmoset Toolbag.

In the next chapter, you will learn about the process of exporting materials for the game engine.

CHAPTER 18

Integration with Unreal Engine 4

Substance Painter was first widely adopted by the game industry. Substance has a well-defined workflow as well as direct integration with modern game engines such as Unreal Engine, Unity, and CryEngine. We will focus primarily on Unreal Engine as our target engine in this chapter.

Unreal Engine is a popular game engine preferred both by AAA Studios and by Indie Studios for developing their games. Big titles like *Mortal Combat 11, Darksiders III, Batman Arkham* series, *Ace Combat 7, Gears 5, Borderlands 3, Star Wars Jedi: Fallen Order, The Outer Worlds*, etc., were made in Unreal Engine.

So, if you want to learn how to use a modern game engine widely used by studios all over the world, then Unreal Engine is the way to go. Unreal Engine does have an extremely complex architecture that is daunting at first; however, this is a rewarding engine to learn because you can easily land jobs in the game development field if you are well versed in Unreal Engine.

We are not going to dive deep into the daunting world of game development as it is not our main focus here. Rather, we will focus on the important aspect of texture integration with Unreal Engine, exported from Substance Painter in our case. The textures can be from any source, but the process will usually remain the same.

© Abhishek Kumar 2020
A. Kumar, *Beginning PBR Texturing*, https://doi.org/10.1007/978-1-4842-5899-6_18

Exporting to Unreal Engine 4

Exporting to Unreal Engine 4 (UE4) from Substance Painter is similar to what you did in the previous chapters with other software because Substance Painter has a preset for Unreal Engine 4.

To export files for use in UE4, first press Ctrl+Shift+E, which is the shortcut key for exporting a texture. Click the Config drop-down menu and choose Unreal Engine 4 (Packed) from the list (Figure 18-1).

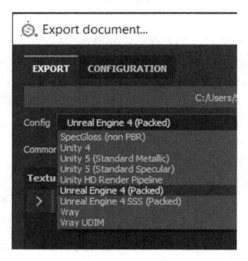

Figure 18-1. *Choosing the UE4 preset*

Now you can go to the configuration to see which maps this preset is using. There you will notice something unique (Figure 18-2).

Figure 18-2. *UE4 export preset configuration*

As you can see, the ambient occlusion (AO), roughness, and metallic maps are being packed into a single texture file into the Red, Green, and Blue channels, respectively. First let's explore why this is done and how it works.

Texture packing is done primarily for optimization purposes. Packing three texture maps into a single map reduces the number of texture maps that need to be loaded into computer memory. This is especially important in the case of games because there is a limited amount of memory available and only so much can be crammed into it at a time. When there are hundreds of assets being rendered along with tons of AI and logic processes, then it is important that memory is saved for more important things. Game engines must render tens and sometimes hundreds of frames per second, so optimization is important. Although this looks like a small number, when there are hundreds or even thousands of assets, things start to stack up quickly.

How does this work? Well, ambient occlusion, roughness, and metalness are all grayscale maps, and the only information they contain is linear. In other words, they store what their value is at any given pixel between 0–1. The same thing is stored by the RGB channels, which is what the value of their respective channels is in any given pixel between 0 and 1.

That is why these AO, roughness, and metalness can be stored in RGB channels of a map because we care only about their values and not about the color information (Figure 18-3).

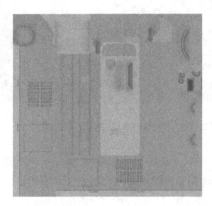

Figure 18-3. *Example of a mixed AO, roughness, and metalness map*

Now let's get back to exporting. Go ahead and change the image format to either png or targa at 16 and then change the document resolution to the 2048x2048 setting. The document resolution for game assets is mostly subjective. It depends on the size of the asset, its importance, its distance from the player, and so on (Figure 18-4).

Once exporting is done, it is time to launch UE4 and set up your material inside UE4.

Figure 18-4. *Export settings*

Importing into Unreal Engine 4

Importing into UE4 is a pretty straightforward process. You can either drag and drop your files directly into the Content Browser of UE4 or use the Import button located in the top-left corner of the Content Browser.

But first let's create a new project. To use Unreal Engine, first launch Epic Games Launcher and then go to the Library and launch whichever engine version you prefer or have installed. The Unreal Project Browser window will open (Figure 18-5).

Figure 18-5. *Creating a new project*

Create a Blank blueprint project with Desktop/Console as the target hardware, with the Maximum Quality setting, and with the No Starter Content setting. Also, choose the destination save folder and name the project. Once everything has been done accordingly, click Create Project. This will launch UE4 with all the settings that you specified.

Once UE4 has launched, you are ready to start working on your project.

Before you import anything, you will create some folders to keep everything organized. To do that, right-click the Content Browser, and from the list that appears click New Folder at the top of the list (Figure 18-6). This will create a new folder and give you the option to name it immediately upon creation. Name this folder **Assets**. Open the folder and create two new folders inside it named **Meshes** and **Materials**.

Now you are ready to import your mesh and textures into UE4. You are going to import the CubeTest mesh and all the textures related to it.

Figure 18-6. *Creating a new folder*

You can import anything into UE4 by either dragging or dropping it inside the Content Browser or by clicking the Import button (Figure 18-7).

Figure 18-7. *Import option*

If you click Import, then the file browser will open allowing you to navigate to your file destination and import your assets. Also, you can drag and drop your assets directly into the Content Browser. Either way, a new window should open allowing you to customize the import options. There are tons of options, and at first this will look overwhelming and rightfully so. But we can leave most of the options on their defaults and change only a few of them.

There's one thing to note here before proceeding. UE4 requires meshes to have a secondary UV channel for baking and storing static lighting information. This usually should be created inside a 3D modeling application. In our case, we did not create one. Luckily, UE4 has an automatic tool for creating Lightmap UVs. This works best with simple meshes and is not that suitable for creating a complex UV layout.

Figure 18-8 shows all the settings for your FBX file.

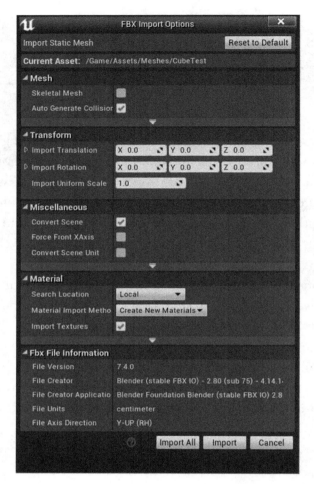

Figure 18-8. _FBX Import Options window_

Some of the settings that you can modify are material settings and
mesh settings. You can see that Material Import Method is set to Create
New Material. If you have kept the texture maps of the mesh in the same
folder as the mesh, then UE4 will automatically search for the textures and
create a rough material setup for you that you can expand upon. As for
the settings related to meshes, click the drop-down arrow next to Mesh to
expand the options and click Generate Lightmap UVs to activate it unless it
is already enabled (Figure 18-9).

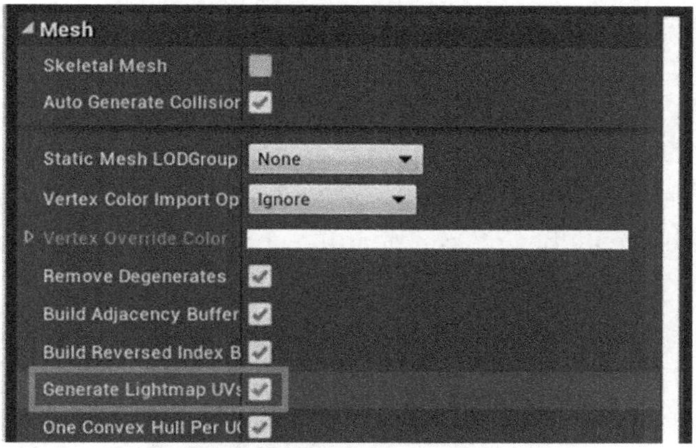

Figure 18-9. *Generate Lightmap UVs setting*

You can double-click your FBX file in the Content Browser to open it in the asset viewer. Here you can edit the properties related to that asset that apply globally to all its instances that you create. See Figure 18-10 and click the UV drop-down menu at the top to see what your UVs look like. You can close this window once you are done exploring; we will return to this later.

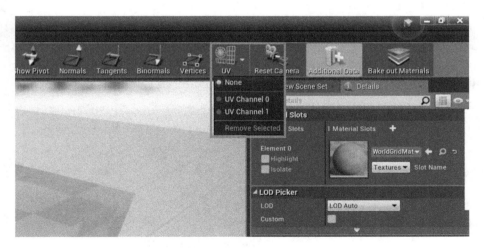

Figure 18-10. *Switching UV channels*

Now you will import the materials. First go to the Materials folder and then click Import or drag and drop them inside this folder. Either way, the textures should come in without any menus appearing. If any warning messages appear toward the bottom right of your screen, just ignore them.

You will set up the material now. First right-click the Content Browser and under the Create Basic Asset heading choose Material (Figure 18-11).

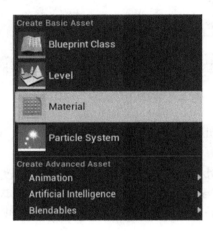

Figure 18-11. *Adding a material asset*

Once the material asset has been created, you can name it. In this case let's call it **M_ExampleCube**. Here *M* is a prefix for material, and naming it ExampleCube will allow us to know whose material is it. Now double-click it, and the material editor will launch.

Figure 18-12. *UE4 material editor*

Figure 18-12 shows the default editor that you will see. Located toward the right side of the window is the Palette, which lists all the nodes that you can drag and drop into the editor. Close this window by clicking the small cross icon. You can access all the nodes by right-clicking the editor, so you don't need the Palette.

Next you will add your image textures into the material editor. To do that, first select all the texture maps that you have imported into UE4 and then drag and drop them into the material editor; this will create texture nodes for them. You now have to connect the correct output pin of the texture nodes to the respective input node of the main material node. First you will arrange them for the sake of convenience. You will keep the base color on top, the normal map just below it, and the mixed roughness, metalness, ambient occlusion (RMA) node at the bottom.

Let's begin with a basic node setup first and then add some details to it. So, here is how we connect. Connect the RGB output pin from the base color node and connect it to Base Color. Then connect the output pin from the normal map node to the normal input pin. For the mixed RMA node, you will make the connections in the following order:

- The Red output will connect to the Ambient Occlusion input.

- The Green output will connect to the Roughness input.

- The Blue output will connect to the Metalness input.

Your final result should look somewhat like Figure 18-13.

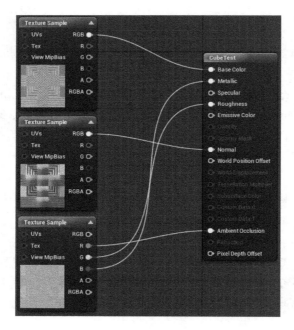

Figure 18-13. *Connection setup for the material*

Your material is set up now, and even though this is a basic setup, this can get the job done when the assets are not too large or don't require too much detail. As you can see, this requires less effort but does not give you options to edit the material. Let's now apply this material to our mesh and see how it looks. Save your material by clicking the Save button at the top-left corner of the screen; after that, you can close the window.

Now, drag and drop the CubeTest mesh from the Content Browser into the scene. There is a default floor mesh placed in the scene, so you can try to place your mesh on that. You can put your mesh several units above the floor mesh; just press the End key on your keyboard to drop your mesh and place it exactly on top of the mesh. Duplicate your mesh a few times by selecting the mesh, holding the Alt key on your keyboard, and dragging it along an axis. After that, drag the material from the Content Browser and drop it on top of one of the meshes. You will see that the mesh will be textured. But only the mesh on which you dropped your material will be textured. Every time you drop a new CubeTest mesh into the scene, the existing ones will not be textured.

But there another way to texture that will bind the material to the mesh. To do this, double-click your mesh, and a new window will open the mesh properties window, which allows you to modify various properties related to the mesh. Here, you will change the material properties (Figure 18-14).

Figure 18-14. *Material properties of your CubeTest*

Currently in the material slot I have WorldGridMaterial applied. Click the drop-down arrow, and in the menu that appears, search for *M_CubeTest* or whatever you have named your material (Figure 18-15).

Figure 18-15. *Searching for the material you created*

Click the material that appears in the search result, and the material will be applied to the mesh. Click Save and close this window. Now you will see that all the CubeTest meshes present in the scene have been textured automatically by your material; plus, the new ones that you create will be textured as well. When you want your mesh to consistently have only one material for every instance that you create, then you can assign texture to it like this.

Now let's see how you can create more complex materials. You will do this by editing your previously created M_CubeTest material. Double-click it to launch the material editor. The first thing that you will do is disconnect the previously created connections. To do this, hover over an input/output pin and Alt+click; this will break the connection. You need to do this for all the connections that you have created so far. Once done, select all the texture nodes and drag them back to create more room for new nodes that we are going to create.

First we will work on our base color. Right-click an empty area in the graph area, and a menu should appear. In its search field, type **cheapcontrast**. It is not necessary to type the full name because entering a few characters will locate what we are looking for, which is CheapContrast_ RGB (Figure 18-16).

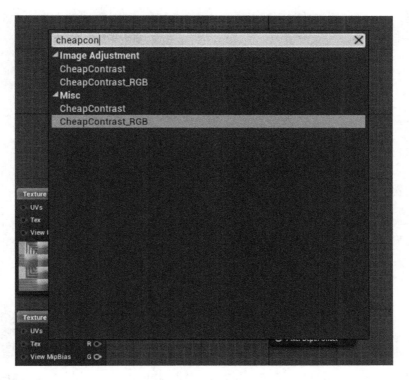

Figure 18-16. *Searching for CheapContrast_RGB*

Click the highlighted node to add it to the editor. Once it has been added, connect the RGB output of base color texture to In(V3). This node allows you to control the contrast of your color. Now you will create a parameter node to control the effect of the CheapContrast node by feeding in numeric values. To do this, you can hold the alphanumeric 1 key and click to add a one-point constant. If you don't remember the shortcut

key, then you can right-click and search for *Constant*. Once it has been
added, right-click it and choose Convert to Parameter from the list. Name
this parameter **Contrast**. Connect the output of the Contrast parameter
to Contrast (S) of the CheapContrast_RGB node. Your setup so far should
look like Figure 18-17.

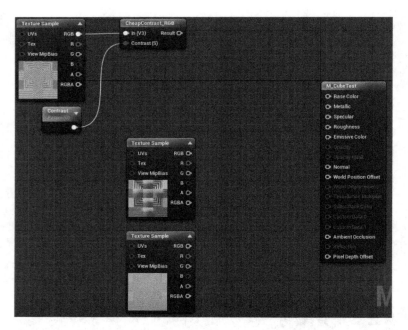

Figure 18-17. *Material setup so far*

Right-click again and search for the Multiply node. Add it to the graph
and then connect the output of the CheapContrast node to the A input of
Multiply. Now you need to add a Constant three Vector. To do that, either
hold 3 and click or right-click and search for *Constant*; then add Constant
three Vector. Right-click and convert this to a parameter and name it
Color. Select the Color node, and its properties should appear on the left
side of the screen under Details (Figure 18-18).

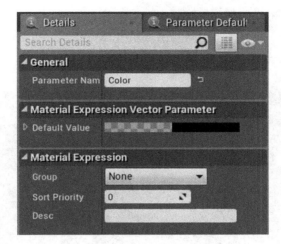

Figure 18-18. *Default parameters of Constant three Vector*

Click the color slot for Default Value, and the color picker will appear. In that window, change all the R, G, and B values to 1. This should make the color white (Figure 18-19).

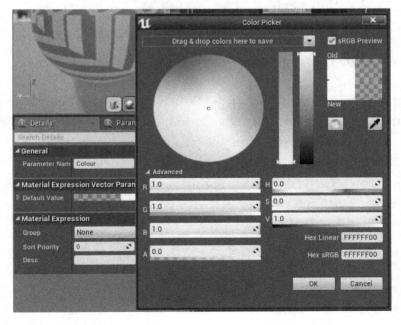

Figure 18-19. *Changing the color value of Constant three Vector*

237

Once you have done that, connect the output of Color to the B input of Multiply. Finally, plug the output of Multiply into the Base Color input of M_CubeTest (Figure 18-20).

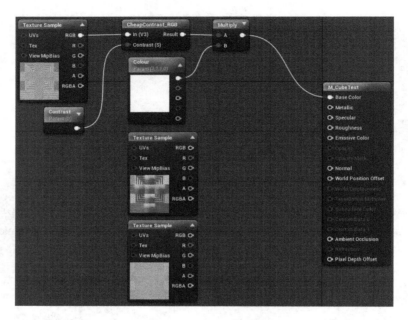

Figure 18-20. *Node network*

You will now work on the normal map. Right-click and search for FlattenNormal. Connect RGB of the normal map to Normal (V3) of the FlattenNormal node. Create a one-point parameter like you did before and name it **Normal_Strength**. Connect its output to the Flatness (S) of FlattenNormal. Then connect the output of FlattenNormal to the Normal input of M_CubeTest (Figure 18-21).

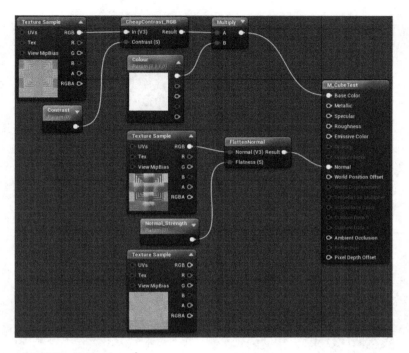

Figure 18-21. *Setup so far*

Now you need to create one parameter named Roughness and one Multiply node. Connect the G output of the MixRMA texture to the A input of Multiply and connect the output of Roughness to the B input of Multiply. Then connect the output of Multiply to the Roughness input of M_CubeTest. Finally, connect the R output of MixRMA to Ambient Occlusion and the B output to Metallic. The material is now set up properly (Figure 18-22).

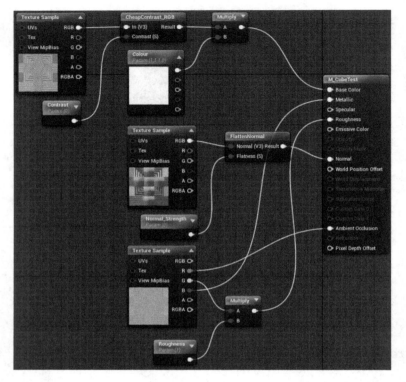

Figure 18-22. *Final material setup*

Click Save and close the window. This will be your master material.
You can duplicate this material and swap the texture maps to create new
materials for other assets. You can actually right-click M_CubeTest and
rename it to **MM_AssetMaster**, but in our simple project this may not be
necessary. But I highly recommend that you rename it to **MM_CubeTest** to
specify that it's the master material.

Right-click MM_CubeTest, choose Create Material Instance, and
rename it to **MI_CubeTest**, which means material instance. The option
Create Material Instance allows you to create and use multiple materials
and edit them individually without affecting the master while inheriting all
the properties of the master material (Figure 18-23).

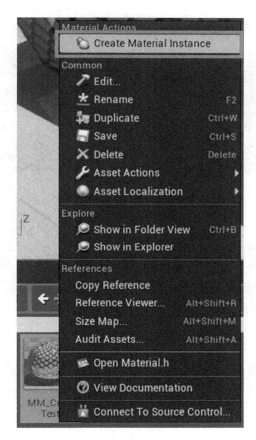

Figure 18-23. *Creating a material instance*

Now you can drag and drop the material on whatever mesh you choose to or you can apply it more permanently like you did before by using the mesh editor. If you double-click the material instance, then a parameter window will open that will allow you to quickly edit the material based on the various parameters you created. You can click the checkbox toward the left side of the name of parameters to enable them (Figure 18-24).

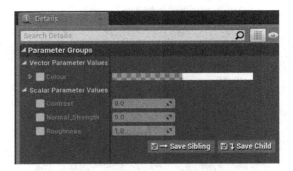

Figure 18-24. *Editable material parameters*

Now play with the values and create variations of your material.

You should now have a clear understanding of how to import your assets into the game engine and how to set up materials. In the next chapter, I will discuss some tips and tricks to speed up your Substance Painter work for the media and entertainment industry.

CHAPTER 19

Tips and Tricks of Substance Painter

In this chapter, you'll explore some tips and tricks that will be helpful in your texturing process.

We will begin by preparing our scene. Let's explore the CubeTest mesh here as well. You will prepare the mesh like you did before by baking all the mesh maps from its high poly version. Then you'll create a new paint layer where you can draw.

Using Brushes and Alphas

In this section, you will see how the alphas of Substance Painter synergize with brushes and learn about everything you can do with them. Let's see how you can play with alphas and use them as height.

First make sure your Paint layer is selected and then disable all the channels except Height. Set the Height value to 0.05 (Figure 19-1).

© Abhishek Kumar 2020

A. Kumar, *Beginning PBR Texturing*, https://doi.org/10.1007/978-1-4842-5899-6_19

Figure 19-1. *Setting up the height*

Then click the Alphas tab in the Shelf. Now pick any alpha. You can also click the mesh to stamp the alpha on your mesh (Figure 19-2).

Figure 19-2. *Example of effect*

If your brush is not acting normally on this mesh and turning to weird angles, then under the brush settings in the Properties window look for Alignment. By default it will be set to Tangent | Wrap, but you should change it to Camera for this example (Figure 19-3).

Figure 19-3. *Changing the brush alignment*

You can change the size of the brush either by using the brush properties or by pressing the [or] key, which will decrease and increase the size of the brush, respectively.

If your brush is not getting as large as you want, then under the brush settings look for Size Space. By default, this option should be set to Object, but you can change it to Viewport. This will allow you to adjust the size of the brush based on your viewport (Figure 19-4).

Figure 19-4. *Changing the size space of your brush*

This was a simple example, so now let's see how to use alphas to create a brand logo.

First, you need a new Paint layer. Activate the Color, Height, Metallic, and Roughness channels in the layer. Set the values of these channels according to Figure 19-5.

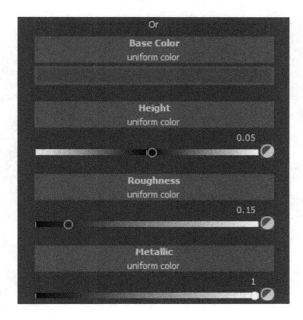

Figure 19-5. *Paint settings*

You don't need to commit to these values exactly; you can certainly create your own variations.

After that, go to the Alpha settings and search for *Band Half Rounded*. Click it to choose it as your alpha. Then under the Alpha settings set Hardness to 1, if it's not already. And set Band Width to 0.75 (Figure 19-6).

Figure 19-6. *Alpha settings*

With all these settings, stamp the alpha anywhere on your mesh. Next search for *Font Libre Baskerville* in the Alpha settings. Click it to apply it as your font. Under the Alpha properties, you will see a text field where you can enter the text you want to have. Also, change Type from Regular to Bold, which should be under the Alpha settings as well. Now in the text field, you can type anything you'd like. For this example, I will change the color to a yellowish tone and create some text, as shown in Figure 19-7.

Figure 19-7. *Example of text*

After you have written what you want, switch from Brush to Eraser. Once again, under Alpha, search for *Font Libre Baskerville* and click it. You will see that the Eraser tool will now display the alpha. In the text field, enter **ENCLAVE** and set Type to Bold. Now you can make your eraser larger and use it on the larger green region of the logo that we are creating. Position your brush and click to get a result similar to Figure 19-8.

Figure 19-8. *Final design*

Creating Stitches

Now you'll learn how you can create stitches in Substance Painter. First delete/disable the layers below unless it is a fresh new scene. Then apply the Leather Medium Grain material to your mesh and set the scale to 6. Now create a Paint layer with the Color, Height, and Roughness maps active. Set the values according to Figure 19-9.

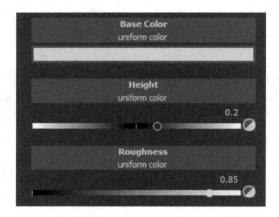

Figure 19-9. *Paint settings*

Then in the Alpha settings, search for *Stitch Generator* and click to choose it as your alpha. Next, in the Alpha settings, expand the Line heading, and you will see several parameters that you can edit. Modify the Scale Y parameter to be 1 and change Scale X to be 0.02. Scroll up to go to the Brush settings and increase the spacing to 110. Your brush is now ready to paint stitches. Click and drag your mesh to see the effect, as shown in Figure 19-10.

Figure 19-10. *Stitches example*

Tip   To draw straight lines, click once to draw one stitch; then hold Shift without moving your camera or mesh, and a straight line will appear from that point to the location of your cursor. Now if you click in another place, the stroke will follow a straight line to its target. Also, if you hold Ctrl+Shift, then your line will snap to 5-degree angles, allowing you to have more accuracy.

Creating Damage Using the Height Channel

Let's see how to utilize the Height channel to create a damage effect. To do this, first you need to create a Fill layer with the Color, Height, Roughness, and Normal channels active. Then choose a brick material from the Shelf that you want to use. If you don't have a brick material, then you get some for free from Substance Share, or you can buy some premium ones from web sites such as Substance Source, GameTextures.com, Poliigon.com, etc. Once you have acquired a brick material and installed it, then drag and drop it from the Shelf to the Base Color slot (Figure 19-11).

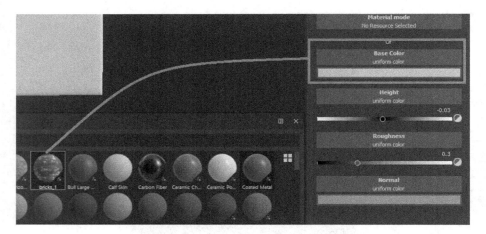

Figure 19-11. *Dropping the material to the base color of the Fill layer*

Drag and drop the material to other channel slots as well, and those slots will automatically take the correct maps from the material. Also, adjust the scaling of the Fill layer according to your needs. Now for the brick's Fill layer; you can set the height to be -0.04. Your setup should look similar to Figure 19-12.

Figure 19-12. *Setup of the Fill layer*

Now create another Fill layer with the Color, Roughness, Height, and Normal channels active. To fill the channels of this layer, you will use one of the default Plaster materials that ships with Substance Painter. Like you did before, you just need to drag and drop the material to the slot of all the active materials except Height. For the Plaster layer, set the height to 0.06. Also, don't forget to set the scaling of the layer accordingly.

One thing to note here: make sure that the Plaster layer is on top of the Brick layer as normally plaster is applied on top of bricks. You can use the Height channel to artificially increase their heights so that they appear to *not* be at the same height level. As of now, only the Plaster layer is visible, so you can't tell what the Height channel is doing.

Let's add a black mask to the Plaster channel and then add the Surface Worn smart mask to it.

Select the Mask Editor sublayer under the mask slot to edit its properties (Figure 19-13).

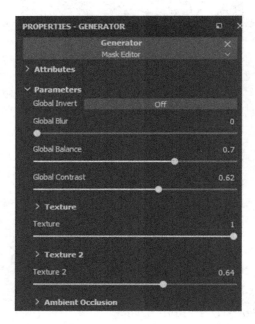

Figure 19-13. *Mask settings*

You can adjust the parameters in any way that looks good to you, but in the end you should have a result similar to Figure 19-14.

Figure 19-14. *Final result*

I hope that after reading this book, you have all the knowledge you need to do PBR-based texturing; in this book, you went from the fundamentals to an expert level. You are now able to integrate PBR textures into your production process and integrate Substance Painter with standard 3D modeling and rendering applications such as Maya and Blender. Congratulations!

Index

A

Albedo map, 36
Allegorithmic's Substance
    Painter, 1
Alpha settings, 247–249
Ambient occlusion (AO)
    map, 37, 85, 223
Anchor points
  baker settings, 146
  Edge Wear generator, 151
  fill layer settings, 147, 149
  generator settings, 150
  micro details settings, 152, 153
  normal map stamps, 148
  procedural operation, 143
  project settings, 145
  referencing anchored
    layer, 154
  removing, Alpha slot, 147
  result, 155
  under layer, 151
  user-defined references, 143
  windows list, 154
Application programming
    interfaces (APIs), 15
Auto stitcher, 124, 125

B

Bake Mesh Maps button, 32, 81, 82
  common parameters, 83–85
  window, 83
Baking maps, 8
Bitmap/traditional texturing, 45
Blender, integration
  adding shaders/nodes, 195
  adding Sun lamp, 199
  connecting nodes, 197
  cycles render device, 201
  EEVEE render engine, 187
  GPU, 202
  GUI, 188
  image texture node, 191, 196
  material parameters, 190
  node setup, 198
  render created, 203
  render Image option, 200
  scene properties, 200
  shader editor, 194
  splitting workspace, 192
  switching, 188
  UV unwrapped model, 189
  viewport type, 193
Blending modes, 93

© Abhishek Kumar 2020
A. Kumar, *Beginning PBR Texturing*, https://doi.org/10.1007/978-1-4842-5899-6

Blur filter, 110, 111

Brushes
    Alphas tab, 244
    changing alignment, 245
    Paint layer, 243
    settings, 247
    size space, 246

Bump map, 36

C

Caustic sampler, 159

Central processing unit (CPU), 55

Clone tool, 75

Computer graphics (CG)
    APIs, 15
    film, 16
    forensic and medical
        animation, 19, 20
    gaming, 16, 17
    history, 15
    picture elements, 13
    pixel representation, 14
    3D, 14
    visualization, 17
    web design, 20

D

Damage effect, Height Channel
    Fill layer, 252
    mask settings, 254
    PBR-based texturing, 255
    setup, 253

Diffuse maps, 36

Dirt generator, 119–122

Displacement map, 37

Document resolution, 79

Dripping Rust generator, 124

E

Eraser tool, 74

Exporting files, Substance Painter
    Blender, 176, 177
        configuration tab, 178
        emissive/height
            channels, 181
        image format menu, 179
        Normal map output type, 180
        output channel, 180
        templates, 178
    Marmoset Toolbag, 184
        image parameters, 186
        MetalRough option, 185
        PBR SpecGloss, 184
    Maya, 181
        Arnold 5 (AiStandard), 182
        Config presets list, 182
        export settings, 183

F

Filters
    Blur, 110, 111
    dragging/dropping, 107, 108
    HSL Perceptive, 113, 114
    manual applying, 106

MatFinish, 108–110
MatFx Edge Wear, 116, 117
MatFx Rust Weathering, 115, 116
Sharpen, 112
Transform, 115
Firefly filter, 159
Forensic and medical
 animation, 19

G

Game engines, 28, 29
Game texturing, 28
 modern *vs.* traditional, 6
 vs. movies, 6
 workflow, 5
Gaming industry, 2, 4, 5
Generators
 auto stitcher, 124, 125
 dirt
  add generator, 120
  generator window, 120, 121
  parameters, 121, 122
  setup, 119
 dripping rust, 124
 effects, 118
 Mask Builder–Legacy and Mask
  Editor, 125–127
 metal edge wear, 122, 123
 typical setup, 118
Graphical user interface(GUI)
 2D/3D aspects, 65
 Layer Stack window, 62
 Properties window, 63

Single-channel mode, 64
Substance Painter, 59
Texture Set List window, 61
Texture Set Settings window, 61
viewport settings, 63
Graphics processing unit (GPU), 55
GPU *vs.* CPU, 55, 56

H

Hardware configuration, 7, 57
HDRI environment, 158
High-performance computing
 (HPC), 57
HSL Perceptive filters, 113, 114

I, J, K

Inorganic/object modeling, 24
Iray renderer, 158

L

Layers
 adding folder, 93
 operations, 91, 92
 paint and procedural data, 90
 types, 91
Lookup tables (LUTs), 68
Low/high poly models, 42
 exploded mesh, 168
 naming mesh parts, 167
 overlapping, 166
 z-fighting, 166

M

Marmoset Toolbag, integration
   final render, 219
   GUI, 215
   input type, 217
   material creation, 216
   selecting Sky, 218
Mask Builder–Legacy and Mask
      Editor generator, 125–127
Masks
   adding levels, 103
   black, 94
   Brush tool, 100
   color selection, 96
   container, 95
   cube example, 94
   fill effect, 101, 102
   inverting, 104
   Polygon Fill tool, 96
   tools and effects, 98, 99
Materials, 89, 90
MatFinish filters, 108–110
MatFx Edge Wear filters, 116, 117
MatFx Rust Weathering
      filters, 115, 116
Maya, integration, 203
   aiStandardSurface shader, 206
   assigning, new material, 205
   attribute editor, 207, 209
   Bump Mapping input, 211
   color space, 210
   files attribute, 208
   final Render, 214
   HDRI SkyDome light, 213

   imported model, 204
   metalness icon, 212
   Render Node window, 208
   roughness input, 210
   Shelf, 213
   3D model, 203
   use type, 211
Mesh maps
   ambient occlusion, 87
   curvature, 88
   geometry information, 86
   SSS effect, 88
   surface details, 85
Metal Edge Wear generator, 122, 123
Modeling, 23

N

Normal map, 37
Normal map format, 80
Notable game companies, 3, 4

O

Offline rendering/
      Pre-rendering, 187
Opacity/transparency map, 36
Organic modeling, 24

P

Paint tool, 74
PBR metallic-roughness
      workflow, 37
PBR shader, 56

PBR specular-glossiness
        workflow, 37
Physically based rendering (PBR)
    approach, 27
    Substance Painter, 1
    textures, 27
    texture science, 27
    video game industry, 1
Polygon Fill tool, 75, 97
Portfolio-ready image, 11
Procedural maps, grunges, 9
    baker setting, 128, 129
    patterns, high
        bricks, 132
        layer properties, 130
        result, 131
        Warp filter, 131, 132
    patterns, masks, 137
        Fabric layer settings, 134, 135
        Fill layer parameters, 133
        Fill result, 134
        Gold leaves layer, 137
        result, 136
        texture parameters, 135, 136
    procedural images
        Height mode, 139
        material parameters, 137, 138
        Perlin noise parameters, 140
        result, 141
        texture parameters, 138, 139
    project creation, 127, 128
Procedural texturing, 43, 44
Production pipeline, 22
    animation, 25

CG live integration, 26
    dynamics, 25
    lighting, 25
    modeling, 23
    rendering, 26
    rigging, 25
    stages, 22
    tasks, 23
    UV map, 24
Projection tool, 74

Q

Quixel suite, 45, 47

R

Rasterization, 14
Real-time/online rendering, 187
Rendering, 26, 187
Rendering (Iray)
    camera settings, 161
    display settings, 160
    environment settings, 160
    post-processing effects, 158
    sample, 159
    settings window, 158, 159
    shader settings, 162, 163
    viewport settings, 162
Resource/asset shelf
    categories, 66, 67
    LUTs, 68
    Substance Painter settings, 69
Roughness, metalness, ambient
        occlusion (RMA), 231

S

Self Occlusion, 85
Sharpen filters, 112
Smart masks, 97, 98
Smudge tool, 75
Specular map, 36, 39
Stitches, creation, 250, 251
Substance Alchemist, 50, 51
Substance Designer, 52, 53
Substance Painter, 47
   anchors, 143
   anchor system, 10
   designer, 48
   export files, 165
   .fbx type, 165
   industry standard, 48
   internal rendering, 10
   library, 49
   procedural workflow, 48
   project, set up, 8
   tips/tricks, 11
   viewport, 8
   workflow, blender, 169
      default exporter window, 170
      export settings, 171
      geometries tab/smoothing
        option, 172
      material editor, 173
      visibility off/on, 169
   Maya, 174
      export window, 174
      selection window, 175

Substance Source, 49, 50
Substance suite, 7, 45
   sectors, 22
   texturing tools, 21
Substance Suite package, 49–53
Subsurface scattering
   (SSS), 39, 88

T

Texture mapping, 24, 39
Texture pipeline, 40, 41
Texturing
   artists, 34
   drawback, 43
   game, 37
   game asset, 32, 33
   game engine/studio
      workflow, 35
   PBR, 31
   3D painting applications, 44, 45
   2D painting applications, 45
   types, 36, 43
   workflow, 31, 32
Three-dimensional (3D) computer
   graphics, 14
3D model
   file location, 78
   new project window, 77, 78
   project configuration, 79, 80
3D texturing. software, 47
Transform filters, 115

U

Unreal Engine 4 (UE4)
  exporting
    AO, 223
    configuration, 222, 223
    settings, 224
    texture packing, 223
  importing
    CheapContrast_RGB, 235
    color value, 238
    connection setup, 232
    creating, material
      instance, 241
    CubeTest, 233
    default parameters, 237
    editable material
      parameters, 242
    FBX Import Options
      window, 228
    folder, creation, 226
    Lightmap UVs setting, 229
    material asset, 230

    material editor, 231
    material setup, 236
    MixRMA texture, 239
    MM_CubeTest, 240
    new project,
      creation, 225
    node network, 238
    option, 227
    searching materials, 234
    switching uv channels, 229
Unwrapping, 24, 35
UV mapping, 31, 35
UV unwrapping, 45

V, W, X, Y, Z

Vertex, 35
Viewport navigation
  functionality shortcuts, 73
  settings, 72
  shortcut keys, 71
  tools, 74–76
  tool selection, 72